LY SIENKIEWICZ'S
BELOVED BALTIMORE
ALBUM QUILTS

25 Blocks • 12 Quilts • Embellishment Techniques

Minnie Jackson
Dunedin, Florida
July 17, 2001

Elly Sienkiewicz with Mary K. Tozer

C&T PUBLISHING

Text, Photography, and Artwork copyright © 2010
by Eleanor Patton Hamilton Sienkiewicz

Publisher: Amy Marson
Creative Director: Gailen Runge
Acquisitions Editor: Susanne Woods
Editor: Lynn Koolish
Technical Editors: Sandy Peterson and Gailen Runge
Copyeditor/Proofreader: Wordfirm Inc.
Cover Designer: Kristen Yenche
Book Designer: Christina D. Jarumay
Production Coordinator: Jenny Leicester
Production Editor: Alice Mace Nakanishi
Illustrator: Aliza Shalit
Photography: Christina Carty-Francis and Diane Pedersen
of C&T Publishing, Inc., unless otherwise noted
Published by C&T Publishing, Inc., P.O. Box 1456,
Lafayette, CA 94549

Library of Congress Cataloging-in-Publication Data

Sienkiewicz, Elly.
[Beloved Baltimore album quilts]

Elly Sienkiewicz's beloved Baltimore album quilts : 25 blocks,
12 quilts, embellishment techniques / Elly Sienkiewicz with
Mary K. Tozer.
p. cm.
ISBN 978-1-57120-848-4 (softcover)

1. Appliqué--Patterns. 2. Patchwork--Patterns. 3. Album
quilts--Maryland--Baltimore. I. Tozer, Mary K. II. Title.
TT779.S5422 2010
746.46--dc22
2010014155

Printed in China
10 9 8 7 6 5 4 3 2 1

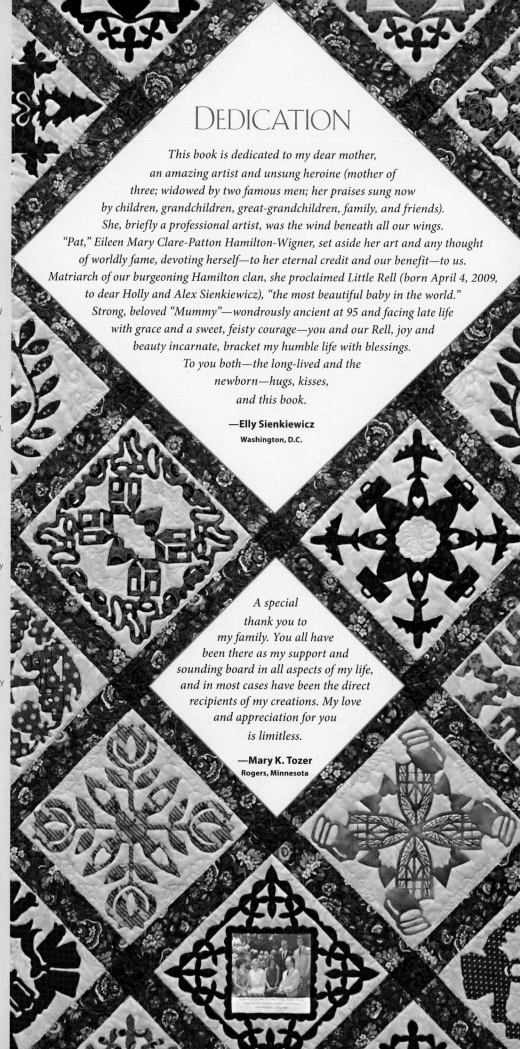

DEDICATION

*This book is dedicated to my dear mother,
an amazing artist and unsung heroine (mother of
three; widowed by two famous men; her praises sung now
by children, grandchildren, great-grandchildren, family, and friends).
She, briefly a professional artist, was the wind beneath all our wings.
"Pat," Eileen Mary Clare-Patton Hamilton-Wigner, set aside her art and any thought
of worldly fame, devoting herself—to her eternal credit and our benefit—to us.
Matriarch of our burgeoning Hamilton clan, she proclaimed Little Rell (born April 4, 2009,
to dear Holly and Alex Sienkiewicz), "the most beautiful baby in the world."
Strong, beloved "Mummy"—wondrously ancient at 95 and facing late life
with grace and a sweet, feisty courage—you and our Rell, joy and
beauty incarnate, bracket my humble life with blessings.
To you both—the long-lived and the
newborn—hugs, kisses,
and this book.*

—Elly Sienkiewicz
Washington, D.C.

*A special
thank you to
my family. You all have
been there as my support and
sounding board in all aspects of my life,
and in most cases have been the direct
recipients of my creations. My love
and appreciation for you
is limitless.*

—Mary K. Tozer
Rogers, Minnesota

ACKNOWLEDGMENTS

To those from around the world who, together, have brought *Elly Sienkiewicz's Beloved Baltimore Album Quilts* to life: Bravo!

Thank you from the bottom of my heart. Thank you, Mary: Mary Tozer made possible—by her offer and delivery of organization—the expansion from one Friendship Album, *Happiness Is in the Journey*, to a traveling show and book. She gave each of us the joy of working with a truly honorable, relentlessly responsible, and cheerful leader. She was group leader of two teams and worked directly with these equally devoted and capable leaders: June Purpura; Tresa Jones and Kelly Kout; Kathy Dunigan; Elinor Burwash and Sandra Rochon; Marla Landt; Lynda Weingart and Marguerite Connolly; Susan Kurth; Suzanne Louth; Marjorie Farquharson, Susan Hart, and Marjorie Lydecker; and Bette Augustine.

Each volunteer for appliqué and each professional setter and quilter (credited in the Gallery on pages 12–22 and in About the Needleartists on pages 116–123) stitched these quilts through with love and talent. I can never fully express my gratitude. Thank you to professional stitcher Holly Sweet for setting quilts together; to professional quilters Cheryl Bowers, "Quiltin' Bill" Fullerton, Linda James, Diane Kirkhart, Susan Mallette, Sue Nickels, Merrily Parker, Gayle Ropp, Connie Tabor, the brokered Amish quilters, and quilt brokers Bellwether Dry Goods. Thank you to my assistants Mary Fox and Teri Young, and to my graphic artists Leona Lang and Evelyn van der Heiden. Thank you to my patrons Judy and Tom Morton and Atsuko Griffin. You, one and all, have affirmed the gift of community and added beauty to the world. Thank you, Bette Augustine, Appliqué Academy administrator and friend.

All the needleartists were asked, "Why has the current Baltimore Album revival lasted so long?" Lynne Huneault's answer, below, evokes a magic that rings true. We have each felt history past and present, our steady companion, as we stitched. The future will surely feel wonder, looking into these quilts, sensing there our presence. May Lynne's words symbolize Mary's and my gratitude to each one who so lovingly led and stitched the quilts in *Elly Sienkiewicz's Beloved Baltimore Album Quilts*.

I believe that Baltimore Album Quilts conjure up the deepest recesses of a woman's heart and soul, plain and simple. That is why, in my opinion, they endure through the ages, through the years, and through the generations. Looking at a Baltimore Album Quilt block conjures up an image of a woman hunched over a piece of cloth for hours, a needle and thread in hand, as she works and coaxes and molds tiny bits of fabric into shapes that are so much more than the sum of their parts. They are a reflection of something inside of her, of a piece of her heart.

I do think that stitching contemplatively, thoughts "off someplace," trying to find ourselves, always leads us back in time. The Baltimore Album Quilts touch women in a particular way. They reflect the little hidden secrets of a woman's heart (which is as deep as the ocean, as they say), and when we look at one of these quilts, it's almost as if we can see those little glimmers of soul between the stitches.

—Lynne Huneault, needleartist

Thank you, Dear Editor, Lynn Koolish, and C&T, who has captained my journey for seventeen of twenty books. Bravo! Thank you, Dear Reader, and all who are able to enjoy in person the exhibition this book catalogs. Thank you to my loyal sponsors: C&T Publishing, The Appliqué Society, Bernina of America, Hobbs Bonded Fibers, YLI Corporation, P&B Textiles, DMC Corporation, and Sakura of America. Thank you, dear, venerable Mummy, for staying the course at 95 and still caring so about all of us who are privileged to love you. Thank you, Dear Children—you have always brought us indescribable joy. And thank you, my Beloved. I cannot imagine such joy without you. You have always given me courage and made the impossible possible.

TABLE OF CONTENTS

Antebellum Albums

It is early September—days are still summer-hot, nights cool, and change blows with the breezes. Dry leaves scudded along the deck this evening, their crisp rustle dancing in fall's breaking news. Summer's sweet perfume of tomatoes, peaches, cantaloupe, and corn wafts in the air—mid-Atlantic bounty, farm-stand fresh—but the last of it infused our supper, filling us with gratitude. It is now the midnight here at the house we rent out all season and then recapture on weekends, as the vacationers retreat. Here at the edge of the sea, waves crash on the shore, waves as repetitious as the tides, waves rolling out an ancient lullaby. Labor Day is tomorrow. We're just down to Delaware via New Jersey, where each month love and duty call me home to my beloved mother. She, about to turn 95, is sweetly proud of her longevity, despite life's hardships.

I've just awoken in the dark. The majestic sea sound pulled me from sleep, pulled me to wake and write, enveloped in night's stillness. Its magic lifts me from dream-realms to practical thoughts—this book to be written. I did not expect to write yet another book on Baltimore's antebellum Album Quilts. *Albums* because they are collections of different quilt blocks, often appliquéd by many hands.

Wondrously close, the sea pounds audibly. I consider why this vintage style captures quiltmakers once again, on such a scale of time and distance as to be dubbed a "quilt revival." Quilted Albums of historic and artistic fame flourished with inscribed dates from 1844 to 1856 in Baltimore City, Maryland. This current Baltimore Album revival movement (1981 to present) spans seas and presses on past three decades in duration. Perhaps the sea is an apt metaphor for the original Baltimores—rare among historic quilt genres, this rich art style remains potent and strong, like a force of nature. And no, I didn't expect that this classic style would still fascinate me, long decades after I had first met her. Nor did I expect that, like ripe, married love, after all these years she can still surprise and delight with revelations about character, not recognized before. Nor could I have foreseen the dear companionship of so many like-minded souls on this, our decades-long happiness journey, Album-led.

Album revival joy, that unexpected endurance of joy, keeps me awake tonight. From whence comes this style's abiding comfort, so oft expressed by faithful stitchers? From whence comes this genre's power to propel modern needlewomen to the outer edges of human capacity? Individuals in any era rise to great heights. Antique quilts in many styles are housed in prestigious museums. So are select contemporary quilts. But the Baltimore Albums came to light as a recognizable style produced in impressive numbers, in a dozen-year span, and in a circumscribed area. They are among the most artistic quilts. Indeed they are eye-catchingly beautiful—they stop us short with that beauty, bulldoze us with the skill that has gone into them. Women who made them hungered to express themselves at a very high standard. In doing so they speak eloquently, but without words. We respond, souls uplifted by that beauty.

Our bygone needlesisters' quilts are uniquely reflective of America's culture mid-nineteenth century. They are love letters, devotions, reflections of faith, journals, romantic marriage announcements of a love match made in a free land. They are like the morning paper—with political statements, news of war—monuments stitched and memorials made. They are a pictorial history of social revolution (abolition, temperance, women's rights); of a nation of newcomers moving west (and leaving many a young Baltimore woman with less chance of marrying); of a nation much caught up in the religious fervor of the Second Great Awakening; of a people in the throes of the Communications Revolution (semaphore, telegraph, portable press) and the Industrial Revolution (reflected in picture blocks of steel-spined steamships and railroad trains). Industry herself is almost personified in the one-layer appliquéd cogwheels, called, in nearby Pennsylvania, Wheel of Progress blocks.

Antebellum Albums act as a snapshot of their times, arguably richer even than realistic pictures and simply decorative designs because they incorporate a common symbolic tongue. (A symbol, as you know, is a visible sign of something invisible.) Greek/Roman, Hebraic, and Christian symbolism (symbols of Western civilization) and that of the fraternal

 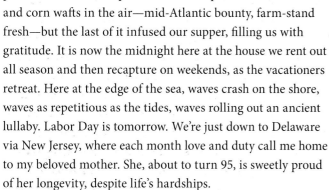

orders has caught our eye in these quilts. These orders are far less pervasive today than back then, yet some symbols remain familiar: A cornucopia, our Thanksgiving symbol, even today represents all the blessings we are given. The linked three-chain (ensconced on Odd Fellow buildings or on tombstones) and a triple-looped bow for friendship, love, and truth are visible metaphors for our obligations one to another. Perhaps these loops of interconnection, passed down, are why you understand just what a modern quilter means by, "I don't want to be a 'weak link' in our raffle quilt; I'll get my block done tonight!" Album Quilt symbols are coterminous with symbols on the era's gravestones, for this is the symbolism of classic and biblical virtues. Similar virtues are reflected in the most literal of symbols, the written word, in the Albums—symbols stitched in cloth, carved in stone:

Here on cloth:

In the pure home of tearless joy
Earth's parted friends shall meet
With smiles of love that never fade
And blessedness complete.

—1847 needlework inscription

Here in stone:

Dearest Mother, thou hast left us
And thy loss we deeply feel.
But 'tis God that hath bereft us,
He shall all our sorrows heal.

—1852 grave inscription

Baltimore's Daughters

The old Baltimore's fame replays today. Seemingly for decades, a revivalist Album annually takes top prize at an international quilt show. We moderns are held, though, by the sense that the Old Ones are more than their visible beauty. We stitch our homage as we stitch our fascination. Our revivalist Albums are old Baltimore's Daughters. So many of our themes are the same as theirs: family, faith, love of country, war, history, marriage, love of beauty, gratitude. Making such a quilt, even making a block for someone else's quilt, makes us happy. But why? In his "Happiness of the People" speech,* Charles Murray named four criteria as necessary for such happiness. To be the source of deep satisfaction ("happiness"), a human activity must—

- Be important—not trivial
- Require effort—doesn't come easily

- Hold you responsible for the consequences—a kit would not be as satisfying
- Stretch your abilities—pull you to a higher achievement

Dedicated Album Quilt makers find within Baltimore—a block, a quilt—a virtual calling. Murray deems a "calling" necessary for happiness. He also concludes that there are only four institutions through which human beings achieve deep satisfaction in life: family, community (can be widely scattered), vocation (can include avocation), and faith. Is this not the stuff of so many quilters' lives?

Contemporary love for and emulation of the antebellum Baltimores reflects something thirsted for, longed for, in today's industrialized world. As a genre now relearned, as a modern quilt movement, Baltimore's Daughters are again fed by volunteer communities. We know them: guilds, bees, classes, conferences, books authored by one but illustrated by many stitched contributions, exhibitions, quilt shows. And like their mothers, Baltimore's Daughters are again achieving artistic notoriety. Individuals who aspire to make great art, to leave it in testament, a gift of beauty by which they will communicate with hearts yet unborn, are today among those drawn to this quilt genre. One source of the movement's power is surely communal support and appreciation for these daughters. Another source of the movement's power must equally be the happiness brought thereby to their makers.

In his book *Human Accomplishment*, Charles Murray asks: What art produced today will be considered great in 150 years? He argues that for a work of art to have meaning for the future, it must reflect, must be motivated to some degree, by something in it of the "transcendental goods." One of the unique characteristics of the Baltimore genre is that it is not merely high craft and art, not merely a reflection of its time and place—but it is also a deeper, symbolic reflection of some "transcendental goods." Murray defines these goods as the search for meaning, for truth, and for beauty; the search for Aristotelian happiness through the habit of virtue. He proposes "that [high] artistic achievement uses the ideals of the transcendental goods as source material. In some cases, as inspiration." We see this reach for virtues not only in the appliquéd symbols but also in antique quilt inscriptions such as the following, courtesy of Nancy Kerns:

This patch though trifling it may seem
Compassion, friendship, and esteem
Mingling with many as a token,
That friendship's ties are yet unbroken.

* "The Happiness of the People," by Charles Murray, The 2009 Irving Kristol Lecture at the American Enterprise Institute (www.aei.org).

AUTHOR'S PREFACE   7

That they capture something more enduring, more spiritual, is one strong reason for the popularity of the Baltimore genre today. Can it truly contribute to its makers' happiness? Yes, for our Albums, the exhibit Baltimore's Daughters satisfies us deeply. Volunteerism in Old Baltimore produced great artwork; volunteerism produced the subject of this book. Volunteerism gave birth to the major traveling exhibition of Friendship Albums that began at Houston's International Quilt Festival 2010 and is moving on to other venues. The collection of quilts pictured herein forms the exhibit Baltimore's Daughters—Friendship Albums for the Future.

How the Exhibit Came About

Its mothers are a close quiltmaking community. The first, Susan Kurth, a loyal quilt class friend, made a teaching block at my request, then continued to make what became the nine blocks of the first Friendship Album, *Through Tufts of Broidered Flowers* (page 15). She chose the blocks from my *Baltimore Beauties* series. We lived half a continent apart. I confessed to be falling behind in the shared task. Susan made all the blocks! But then she gently held me responsible for the setting (me, stitching by Holly Sweet), inking of beautiful snatches of poetry (me), and hired quilting (Cheryl Bowers).

When *Baltimore Elegance* was published, I sought a model with which to teach my favorite blocks. Volunteers from the Appliqué Academy, Appliqué by the Bay, and Heartbeat Quilts offered to stitch. Holly Sweet set it together, and Susan Mallett machine-quilted it, aided by Sue Nickels. (Machine when all the appliqué is by hand? Yes, for ours will surely be remembered as the "classic age" of machine quilting.)

Among the volunteers was Mary Tozer, who offered to stitch the dramatic Clipper Ship medallion center of *Happiness Is in the Journey*. Subsequently she offered to lead that group and help with any organization needed. Her offer held. Other Friendship Album groups sprang spontaneously out of my 2007 teaching. Mary's administrative generosity linked these groups and launched what unexpectedly became something of a movement. Along the way, not only did Mary become fabric cutter and distributor; finisher of orphaned blocks (rare!); and administrator to the group leaders, who themselves were amazing in their generosity of time and talent given, as well as their reliability and efficiency; but she also became cyberspace communicator par excellence. She blessed and united us all with far-north Minnesotan plain speaking and can-do attitude, impeccable responsibility, heartwarming generosity, warmth, and cheer.

The first top, *Friendship's Offering* (page 13), from Calgary, was finished just half a year later after Elinor Burwash and Sandra Rochon proposed it in class. Like a snowball rolling through a downhill snowfield (albeit one of warmth and joy), the concept of Baltimore's Daughters grew quickly. It grew in 2007 as I traveled and taught along the west coast from Canada to California, across the country, and along the east coast from Massachusetts to Florida. Along the way, two of the quilts were made for beloved local teachers, incorporated under the Daughters' umbrella through my Robert Kaufman fabric and Mary's shepherding. You'll follow the Daughters' history better, reading the names and locations, noting capable teams in the Gallery captions (pages 12–22). Bette Augustine, my well-loved Appliqué Academy administrator, looking out at this multiplying family (of which she herself was a stitching member), bought fabric on her own and asked a handful of volunteers to join in making the last-born sister, a small, repeated Wreathed Heart block gem of her own design, to be made with gratitude for our Daughters' fearless leader, Mary Tozer. Bette offered me the privilege of joining with finishing touches of inscribing (my special joy) the top in dedication and gratitude, and of hiring Linda James to quilt it. At the Elly Sienkiewicz Appliqué Academy, 2010, in Colonial Williamsburg, Virginia, Bette and I presented *Verdant Hearts* (page 15, hearts symbolizing our appreciation; green, growing and thriving) to Mary, amidst a standing ovation. Thus may readers long hence know that we joined hands to make these quilts for many reasons, among them fun and love!

These sisters—both the stitchers and the quilts—have led to the Fall 2010 Quilts, Inc., Houston Invitational Exhibition, this C&T Publishing book, and new P&B Textiles fabric. These sister quilts, with friendship names thereon, have become history. In truth, each quiltmaker's strong sense of being participants in history had much to do with bringing these quilts to life. Nine of the quilts were made for me, and after they've traveled and helped me teach, they will be held by their parents for my grandchildren. Suzy Louth, group leader of *Faith, Hope, and Love* (page 22), told me early on, "Elly, you know we are making these quilts for your grandchildren. So we need family pictures, family traditions." She, and perhaps everyone, understood! Those wee innocents and I will forever have warmth and gratitude for this affection.

Making History in Our Ordinary Lives

Why would talented needlewomen self-organize in making Friendship Albums? It makes me think of Alexis de Tocqueville's amazement in 1831 when he reported on the uniqueness of Americans' repeatedly banding together, voluntarily organizing to accomplish something that not one of them could have done alone. Quilters love the challenge of voluntarily doing for others. Part of the Baltimore's Daughters' impetus was friendship, part was pleasure, and much was the joy of industrious productivity. There was also the conviction confirmed by the Old Baltimores, that what we are engaged in is history. I had chosen miniature 8-inch blocks to show how far we'd come in skill, how much we'd learned from Baltimore's "mothers" in the decades-long (1981 to present) Baltimore Album Revival. As we've stitched, we've come to see in the Old Ones a society undergoing revolutionary change, as are we ourselves. As our skill with the needle has grown, so too has our sense that in our Albums we could show a bit more of our own lives, times, and talents to hearts yet unborn. Their understanding, and perhaps ours, would be enriched thereby.

Let's listen a moment to a handful of the group leaders in their own words. In the Patterns section (pages 83–110) are observations of some of the other volunteer appliqué stitchers. Imagine if you and I had inherited this sort of background history with the Old Ones. We would be thrilled to learn what sort of path their makers walked, to learn the makers' ambitions for their quilts and for themselves. We do, indeed, make history in our everyday lives; and do you doubt that one day our quilts too, like the Old Ones, will be considered classics—quilt art that sets a standard for all time?

The Quiltmakers

The 245 volunteer quiltmakers come from 34 states and 4 countries! In addition in the credits are the names of professional quilters (except the Amish brokered quilters, whose names are not provided) and one professional setter, Holly Sweet. Unless otherwise noted, I designed the basic quilt set with borders and the Goose Girl medallions, often leaving the quilt leaders to choose the blocks. The Goose Girl is a rare, but repeated, motif in old Baltimores. The Goose Girl is often walking from a yellow house (symbolically the house of friendship, probably from a meeting of Rebekahs), accompanied by a curly tailed dog (for fidelity) and two geese (the Old Testament's Rebekah made her husband's flocks prosper).

Research makes me believe she is a "Daughter of Rebekah" (the ladies' auxiliary of the Odd Fellows, begun in Baltimore in 1851). Graphed, published dates inscribed Baltimore Albums, at a peak at 1851, implying the influence of the Rebekahs in many of the quilts. The Rebekahs are often in the Albums by way of their symbol, the dove ("Thou shalt be as the dove, and do no one any harm"), and the triple bow knot illustrating the motto "Friendship, Love, and Truth." Baltimore's Goose Girl stars again! For fun I designed her into the center medallions of four of the Friendship Albums.

As in the Old Ones, Goose Girl is recognized always accompanied by a pair of geese and a dog. She visits us quiltmakers in the very friendship hubs where we "raised" our daughters. You'll appreciate hearing how we linked hearts and hands around the world (in family rooms, through cyberspace, and by telephone and email) to make these Friendship quilts.

QUILT LEADERS SHARE THOUGHTS ON THE FRIENDSHIP ALBUM PROJECT

 Faith, Hope, and Love (page 22)

It was my two-fold idea to lead a learning experience for our local The Appliqué Society (TAS) chapter and to contribute something special for Elly's 2010 collection of quilts. Although I led the group, much of the creativity came from my design team of Missy Hartman and Valeta Hensley and from our TAS members with talented fingers and generous hearts.

Elly had mentioned that she would love to use the papercut style with some photo-transfer blocks to blend the old and the new in a twenty-first century Album. We decided to design the blocks using the symbols of modern "ties that bind" today's families together. It was Missy who said, "Since this is to be Elly's quilt, let's ask her how *her* family remains close!" So drawing from the Hamilton-Sienkiewicz traditions, we began with Elly's medallion of family trees, joined by hearts, stitching it to represent love through successive generations. Their family Thanksgiving prayer, holiday celebrations, treasured photos, and "keeping in touch with the kids" set the theme for individual blocks. *Faith, Hope, and Love,* perfect guide words for families through the ages, became our quilt's title.

(Continued on next page)

The result of this adventure is so much more than a lesson and a quilt. Yes, we learned a lot, and we made a lovely quilt, but the best part has been the happiness of being a part of something shared in common. We have laughed, struggled with inside and outside points, munched on cookies, bragged on each others' work, and in the end realized we are a blessed group of friends. Perhaps this is exactly what those first Album makers could have told us. My hope is that our discovery will be the joyous reward for generations of women coming along after we are gone.

—Suzanne Louth

Think of Me, Dear One (page 19)

Think of Me, Dear One—such a lovely sentiment! One that represents, to those of us who made it, a grand and breathtaking quilt to treasure through the years. So many hands, each with a unique story, were a part of making this quilt, from beginner appliquérs to those who have stitched for oh-so-many years. This quilt truly is a mosaic of people. It is much like attending the Elly Sienkiewicz Appliqué Academy—surrounded by such diverse backgrounds, yet we all come together, like-minded, for love of appliqué and each others' company.

Elly had long urged me to lead a quilt that I could use as a teaching tool to teach further afield. She suggested a Friendship Album for the group exhibit Baltimore's Daughters. What fun to select the blocks, choose the fabrics and embellishments, and then mail these kits out in so many directions! My needleartists are a group of stitching friends, some that I taught at one time or another, some that I first made contact with through the academy, and some from an Internet chat group. All of us were eager to be a part of something so grand with Elly!

This quilt idea began in September 2007. Just two years later, in 2009, it was done. What joy it was to receive each finished block back through the mail and to hold in my hands a dear or new friend's stitching! I set the blocks and borders together and was then on to the quilting. I really got to "know" each lady and her block as I lovingly stitched it. I hope that when this quilt is seen through the years, wherever it may travel, the viewer will find joy in the stitches. As for me, a small-town girl from Louisiana, I never could have imagined that my journey with quilting would have taken me on this awesome path. I thank all the ladies who volunteered to help make this quilt a reality. And with all my heart, I thank my dear friends Elly and Mary, for letting me be a part of this fabulous undertaking.

—Kathy Dunigan

Affection's Tribute (page 18)

My sister and I grew up with quilts made by my great aunt, and we loved playing with the scraps she collected in a basket next to her treadle sewing machine. I finally had the opportunity to begin my quilting adventure after serving for 21 years in the U.S. Navy Nurse Corps. Volunteering is part of military service, so when Elly told us of her plans for a new collection of quilts at her seminar in Lewes, Delaware, I signed on as group leader without hesitation. I was thrilled that I had a mission, even though I was retired!

In all, 29 needleartists from 8 states stitched their individual creativity into each splendid block. I was not at all surprised when they would call and ask, "Is it alright if I … ?" Although the blocks were assigned to them, each had a vision for their block that resulted in designs that are classic but original. Some stitched in small, local groups, but we all kept in touch to bring it together.

I hope those viewing *Affection's Tribute* in the future may be inspired to action by our artful appliqué and design, as we each are by the Baltimore Album Quilts of the mid-1800s.

—Kelly Kout

Happy Hours, Sweetly Spent (page 20)

Aspens glitter in every direction as I approach the mountains surrounding Jackson, Wyoming, in autumn. Cresting the Teton Pass gives me a view of the city below, but it is the renewal of friendship that draws me in to the gathering at Quilting in the Tetons the first week of October. For more than a decade, I have been attending Elly Sienkiewicz's classes on Baltimore Album Quilts in Jackson. Every year these intricate blocks and Elly's knowledge of the art and symbolism within them entice me to learn more. Each block she leads us through becomes a pathway to new techniques, honed appliqué skills, and women's history, as well as the time to gather with women of like hearts.

The classes fill with friends from years past as well as welcome new stitchers. It was a vision of the quilt that could be accomplished, as well as the companionship of Elly and those who stitch with her in Jackson, that led me to become the group organizer for this quilt. It has been a delight from the beginning of establishing contact with all the stitchers, choosing the blocks, making kits from Elly's newest fabric line, and then receiving the exquisitely executed blocks from each woman, who so generously gave of her talent and time.

I was inspired each step of the way by the women who made these blocks. Stitchers from nine different states, Utah, North Dakota, Montana, Missouri, Mississippi, Idaho, Colorado, California, and Alaska, volunteered to be part of this project. Distance proved to be no obstacle as we all worked to showcase our skills, providing insight into talents not lost over the generations since the original Baltimore Album Quilts were created. Perhaps our daughters and granddaughters will view these blocks as a window into our gatherings in Jackson. It would be my wish that those who view the quilt see it as a gift of lasting friendship between the stitchers, to Elly, and to those who have the occasion to admire it.

—**Marla Landt**

 Friendship's Offering (page 13)

Friendship's Offering was made with love for our friend Elly Sienkiewicz. We gave our time and talents in each of the blocks, connecting with one another as we share with you our love for the needle. We are grateful to you, Elly, for providing us with the patterns and fabric, and for allowing us to join together with one another. The spirit it contains does not end, as we share our love for all to view. It is given to you as an offering of our continued friendship.

—**Elinor Burwash, co-leader**

Friendship's Offering was created for Elly Sienkiewicz by a group of more than 40 Canadian needleartists to feature a Canadian theme within a Baltimore Album style quilt. The seeds of *Friendship's Offering* were sown at a workshop with Elly at the Fabric Cottage in Calgary, Alberta, in September 2007. Baltimore Album Quilts are rich with history and symbolism, and our goal was to create a version using Canadian themes and images. Research from Elly's previous publications provided blocks suitable for our adaptations, and each needleartist was invited to add her interpretation in the spirit of Canadian friendship.

The provincial and territorial flowers of Canada are presented in bouquets and set in a V to symbolize the flight formation of Canada geese. Each bouquet is wrapped with heritage silk ribbon in the turquoise color of our glacial lakes. Fruit production across Canada is represented in the apples, strawberries, and grapes; the trumpet vine resembles fiddleheads. The lyre represents the harp in the Canadian coat of arms, and the fleur-de-lis was the first heraldic emblem raised in Canada by Jacque Cartier in 1534. One of the most recognized Canadian symbols is the maple leaf, and stylized by Elinor Burwash, it plays a prominent role throughout the quilt. Canadians of all origins are represented in the sprigs of maples leaves in each corner. The dedication and talents of each needleartist are applauded, and the quilt is presented to Elly as an offering of our friendship.

—**Sandra Rochon, co-leader**

A Slice of History

Today is another day. The sound of the refrigerator, punctuated by the ice maker's dropping cubes, drowns out last night's sea sounds. From the porch I see the sky, overcast. No cottony cloud shapes decorate the view; just a still, luminous gauze of gray. The waves were still rough when we took our early swim, but now it is the wind itself singing to me, blowing through the trees, trying to shake out a chorus of drying leaves. This is the quiet sort of day we quiltmakers love, the kind of day whereon our stitches string pearls of thoughts through basted appliqués. On such a soft sort of day we might, in the quiet, think, What is man's relation to the universe? *Or,* How must I live my life? Are these not humanity's most important questions? Surely they are questions that lead us back to Baltimore's Daughters. Thousands of years ago, in the Cradle of Western Civilization, Aristotle noted, "All beauty comes from God." In creating beauty we give comfort and joy, even as we are given it. Philosophically, that helps answer why making revivalist Baltimores makes us happy. But this book is about a specific group of Album Quilts, which themselves seem to be spawning a Baltimore revivalist movement anew. It studies a slice of contemporary history: what we quiltmakers intended and what we have done. We hope that reading this book leaves you happier, that the beauty created here with God-given ability and painstaking care, generously shared, leaves you with a smile!

Elly Sienkiewicz

Eleanor Patton Hamilton Sienkiewicz
October 3, 2009, Lewes Beach, Delaware

Happiness Is in the Journey
(Colloquial Name: *Happiness Journey*), 68″ × 68″, 2007

Made for Elly Sienkiewicz by volunteers from the annual Elly Sienkiewicz Appliqué Academy, Williamsburg, VA; professional stitchers; Heartbeat Quilts' annual Baltimore Seminar, Heartbeat Quilt Shop, Hyannis, MA; and Appliqué by the Bay annual seminar at Mare's Bears Quilt Shop, Lewes, DE. Group leader: Mary K. Tozer; set design, *Happiness Journey* pattern, and inked calligraphy and cartouches by Elly Sienkiewicz; medallion appliqué by Mary K. Tozer; border by Maryann McFee and Kathy Spielman; set together by Holly Sweet; machine-quilted by Susan Mallett with Sue Nickels; quiltmakers/provenance label machine-embroidered by Janice Vaine. Complete list of needleartists is on page 116.

Friendship's Offering
(Colloquial Name: *Canada*),
93″ × 104″, 2008

Made for Elly Sienkiewicz by volunteer long-time class members at the Fabric Cottage in Calgary, Alberta, Canada, and professional stitchers. Group leaders: Elinor Burwash and Sandra Rochon; set design by Elinor Burwash, Sandra Rochon, Wanda Cracknell, Dawn Dick, Karen Osatchuk, and Laurel Frances; border appliqué by Leslie J. Barnes and Andrea Hawkes; stitched together by Elinor Burwash, Wanda Cracknell, Dawn Dick, and Karen Osatchuk; hand-quilted by Diane Kirkhart; quiltmakers/provenance label hand-inscribed by Sandra Rochon with captioning by Evelyn van der Heiden. The quilt was presented to Elly with an accompanying heirloom-appropriate quilt case with history enclosed made by Sandra Rochon. Complete list of needleartists is on page 123.

Our Summer Journey
(Colloquial Name: *Marjorie Lydecker's Quilt*), 83″ × 83″, 2009

Made for Marjorie Haight Lydecker, begun at Heartbeat Quilts, Hyannis, MA, by students of Elly Sienkiewicz and Marjorie Haight Lydecker, a beloved Cape Cod teacher. Group leader: Marjorie J. Farquharson; set designed by Marjorie Lydecker and Marjorie J. Farquharson; set together by Marjorie Lydecker; quilted by Frances Avell Brand, Diane Craft, Audrey Germer, and Marjorie Lydecker; medallion and corner block made using pattern by Jinny Beyer (with permission); border adapted from Bette Augustine's Stars and Flowers Border (with permission). This quilt was made as a surprise gift for dear Marjorie Lydecker, adding to Our Summer's Journey and the girlish fun of secrets! Complete list of needleartists is on page 122.

Verdant Hearts
(Colloquial Name: *Mary Tozer's Quilt*),
48″ × 48″, 2009

Made with thanks and appreciation for Mary K. Tozer. Bette Augustine led this group quilt to honor Mary's monumental contribution to Baltimore's Daughters.

Blocks made by Baltimore's Daughters from around the world; set designed by Bette Augustine from an Elly Sienkiewicz pattern; medallion made by Bette Augustine and Angela Cotter; set together by Bette Augustine; extensive provenance inscriptions by Elly Sienkiewicz; machine-quilted and bound by Linda K. James. Made secretly, it was presented to Mary K. Tozer at The Elly Sienkiewicz Appliqué Academy, February 2010.

Text continues on page 111. Complete list of needleartists is on page 123.

for good close-up: See Quiltmania #81 p17

Through Tufts of Broidered Flowers
(Colloquial Name: *Susan Kurth's Quilt*),
66″ × 66″, 2005–2009

Made between Susan Kurth's home in Oklahoma City, OK, and Elly Sienkiewicz's home in Washington, D.C. Group leader: Susan Kurth chose and appliquéd the blocks as well as choosing poetry quotations for Elly to inscribe on the top; quilt set designed by Elly Sienkiewicz using her first fabric line for Robert Kaufman Fabrics; set together by Holly Sweet; hand-quilted by Cheryl Bowers; quiltmakers/provenance label machine-embroidered by Janice Vaine. More information is on page 121.

Dear Friends Remembered
(Colloquial Name: *Williamsburg Appliqué Academy*),
86″ × 86″, 2009

Made for Elly Sienkiewicz by volunteers predominantly from the annual
Elly Sienkiewicz Appliqué Academy, Williamsburg, VA, and professional
stitchers. Group leader: Mary K. Tozer; medallion center by Emily S. Martin;
set together by Holly Sweet; hand-quilted by Connie M. Tabor; quiltmakers/
provenance label machine-embroidered by Janice Vaine. Quilt designed
by Elly Sienkiewicz with Leona Lang. Complete list of needleartists is on
page 118.

Let Us Be Friends
(Colloquial Name: *California)*,
70″ × 70″, 2008–2009

Made for Elly Sienkiewicz by volunteers from her annual Baltimore Reunion
Seminar at Eddie's Quilting Bee, Sunnyvale, CA, and professional stitchers.
Group leader: June Purpura; set design and Goose Girls Harvest California
Grapes center pattern by Elly Sienkiewicz; medallion by Mary K. Tozer
with Marcia J. Smith; set together by Connie Chapman and Lynn Rodby;
hand-quilted by Sue Nickels; quiltmakers/provenance label machine-
embroidered by Janice Vaine. Quilt designed by Elly Sienkiewicz with
Mary K. Tozer. Complete list of needleartists is on page 119.

Affection's Tribute
(Colloquial Name: *By the Bay*),
68″ × 68″, 2008

Made for Elly Sienkiewicz by volunteers from Appliqué by the Bay annual seminar, Mare's Bears Quilt Shop, Lewes, DE, and professional stitchers. Group leaders: Kelly Kout and Tresa Jones; set design and center pattern Goose Girl Goes Fishing on the Bay! by Elly Sienkiewicz; medallion appliqué by Nancy Kerns; block arrangement, border appliqué, and set together by Tresa Jones; inked medallion calligraphy and cartouches by Elly Sienkiewicz; hand-quilted by Gayle Ropp; quiltmakers/provenance label machine-embroidered by Janice Vaine. Complete list of needleartists is on page 119.

Think of Me, Dear One
(Colloquial Name: *Kathy Dunigan's Quilt*),
69″ × 73″, 2008

Made by volunteer class members (in Turkey and various Canadian and American locations) as a Friendship Album for beloved teacher Katherine Scott Hudgins Dunigan. Kathy led the group, designed the set, appliquéd the center medallion, and quilt and bound this beauty. Complete list of needleartists is on page 120.

Happy Hours, Sweetly Spent
(Colloquial Name: *Jackson Hole*),
82″ × 82″, 2008

Made for Elly Sienkiewicz by volunteers from Elly's Baltimore classes at Quilting in the Tetons, Jackson, WY. Group leader Marla Duenwald Landt also appliquéd the border and the medallion; set design and center pattern Goose Girl Frolics in the Tetons! by Elly Sienkiewicz; stitched together by Pam Ventgen; machine-embroidered quilt provenance label by Janice Vaine. Complete list of needleartists is on page 120.

Sweet Remembrance
(Colloquial Name: *Florida*),
72″ × 72″, 2008

Made for Elly Sienkiewicz by volunteers from Elly's courses at The Old Green Cupboard, Jacksonville, FL. Group leaders: Lynda Feldman Weingart and Marguerite Connolly; set design and center pattern Goose Girls Pick Florida Oranges! by Elly Sienkiewicz; medallion made by Lynda Feldman Weingart and Marguerite Connolly; set together by Holly Sweet; quilted by Bellwether Dry Goods, Lothian, MD; quiltmakers/provenance label machine-embroidered by Janice Vaine. Complete list of needleartists is on page 121.

Faith, Hope, and Love
(Colloquial Name: *Elly's Quilt*),
70˝ × 70˝, 2009

Made for Elly Sienkiewicz by volunteers from Show Me Your Stitches, The
Appliqué Society chapter of Springfield, MO. Group leader: Suzanne Louth,
who also designed, stitched, and shared stash; set design by Suzanne
Louth, Valeta J. Hensley, and Missy Hartman; medallion appliquéd by
Suzanne Louth; India ink and dip-pen calligraphic inscription designed
and executed by Denise Clausen; papercut medallion pattern made by
Elly Sienkiewicz; photo-transfers and typography by Teri Young; borders
by Ruth Rakop and Missy Hartman; machine quilting by Merrily Parker
and "Quiltin' Bill" Fullerton; appliquéd label by Suzanne Louth, Valeta J.
Hensley, and Missy Hartman, who also designed many of the papercut
blocks specifically expressing motifs meaningful to Elly's family life.
Complete list of needleartists is on page 122.

Elly Sienkiewicz's Beloved Baltimore Album Quilts is itself a sort of album, a bound collection a bit like the centuries-old tradition of album book collections. Found on the web: an 1824 Album of a Chinese student come to study in America; an antiquity for sale, it proffers watercolors, poems, and other readings. This book that you hold also intends erudition and entertainment. Among its offerings are glorious photos of the history-making 2010 Baltimore's Daughters Album Quilt Exhibition at the Houston Convention Center in Texas.

Would you like to make *Happiness Is in the Journey,* the Album Quilt that inspired the early twenty-first century's Friendship Album movement? All patterns and the techniques to do so lie within these covers. Does history interest you? Read contemporary Album Quilt makers' musings on the strength and ongoing length of that movement. Enjoy the vintage inscriptions that ornament the pattern pages, seasoning them with the flavor of bygone times. The women who stitched the blocks herein differed in their experience with appliqué. Many have long loved the Albums and were called to embellish and innovate, so their intriguing advanced techniques are included.

How to Use This Book

All the blocks in *Happiness Is in the Journey* are given in the Patterns section (pages 83–110), sized for a background square cut after appliqué to 8½″ × 8½″. If you wish to enlarge the pattern size, enlargement percentages are on page 85.

Are you new to appliqué? Bravo! Welcome! The first patterns are the easiest. They are Cutaway Appliqué blocks, using the simple method that made me an appliquér. Then techniques are added and the blocks increase in challenge, advancing from separate stems and flora to dimensional techniques and multiple layers of fabric. One basic stitch, the tack stitch (page 29), is used for appliqué. Alternatively, Fusible Appliqué (page 60), delightfully easy, is edged with blanket stitch. To begin, choose a simple one- or two-layer block, such as Patterns 2 and 3 (pages 87 and 88).

Wise women differ on preferring Prepared Appliqué, where seams are turned under over freezer paper, or Needleturn Appliqué, where the seam is turned under by your needle, just ahead of stitching. Both methods are taught in Appliqué Basics (pages 28–40).

The first several patterns were designed to be cut and sewn by needleturn out of a single piece of green foliage fabric pinned to the background. This is Cutaway Appliqué, a good place to start.

Tools and Notions

CUTTING

- 5″ fabric scissors (that cut to the point) for cutting appliqué shapes
- 3″ embroidery scissors for cutting into corners or turning under points
- 8″ sewing shears for the traditional cutting of blocks, sashings, and borders
- 5″ paper scissors for cutting templates
- 5″ scissors (strong) for cutting stacked paper, such as multiple templates or Papercut Appliqué designs (Gingher Tailor's Point scissors [G5C] are the best I have found for finely cutting through up to eight layers of freezer paper.)
- Rotary cutter, gridded acrylic ruler, and cutting mat (*optional*) for cutting the blocks, borders, and sashing

PINS, NEEDLES, AND THREAD

Pins

- Fine ball-headed ¾″ pins for appliqué
- 1½″ silk pins or small gold safety pins for holding the appliqué fabric square to the background

Needles

- Sharps needles size #10 or #11 are the traditional needle for Prepared Appliqué where the seam has already been turned under (page 29).
- Milliner's needles size #10 or #11 are ideal for Non-prepared Appliqué. These slightly longer needles facilitate the sweeping under that is required for needleturn. They are sometimes called milliner's straw needles (for sewing flowers on straw hats) or simply straw needles. This needle can be used for all appliqué.
- Crewel or embroidery needles size #9 or #10 for one or two strands of embroidery floss
- Chenille size #24 for up to six strands of embroidery floss
- Chenille size #22 for basic silk-ribbon embroidery

Note: The larger the size number of a needle, the smaller the needle's diameter. Thus a size #12 needle is a finer needle than a size #8.

Thread

- Use a fine thread in a neutral color or in a color matched to the appliqué, not to the background fabric. Excellent are YLI's Silk 100 thread or Mettler 3-ply 50- or 60-weight cotton. YLI makes Elly Sienkiewicz designer thread sets:
- Baltimore Album Set (reds and greens)
- Appliqué Traveler's Set (provides the remaining colors)
- Elly Sienkiewicz's Embellishment Threads—variegated 30-weight

TEMPLATE MAKING

- Freezer paper
- Self-stick paper, uncut label sheets, or contact paper

MARKING AND MEASURING

- Dark and light fabric marking pens
- Fine mechanical pencil
- Pigma .01 pen for inscribing blocks
- Silver or gold Sakura Gelly Roll Pen for tracing around templates; marks both light and dark fabrics
- ¾″-wide masking tape
- Repositionable clear tape
- 6″ ruler: C-Thru ¹⁄₁₀″ grid is excellent
- 8½″ square gridded ruler (see Sources, page 126)
  OR
- Template plastic to make a semiopaque 8½″ × 8½″ square for trimming the finished blocks. Each pattern design image fits within a 7″ × 7″ square. An 8½″ square template makes an 8″ × 8″ finished square when a ¼″ seam allowance is used for piecing, allowing space around each pattern design.

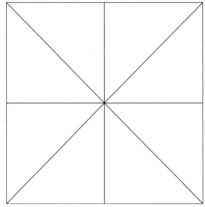

Make an 8½″ × 8½″ square semiopaque plastic template marked with vertical, horizontal, and diagonal centers.

PATTERN TRANSFER

- Lightbox for tracing patterns (page 85)
- Freezer paper for templates and papercuts (pages 83–85)
- 8½″ × 11″ uncut self-stick labels for templates

BASTING

- Clover appliqué pins
- Gluestick
- Roxanne's Glue-Baste-It

PRESSING

- Iron (with a Linen setting)
- Breadboard or other hard ironing surface
- Magic Sizing spray finish
- Paper towels as pressing cloths
- Worn terry-cloth towel on which to iron appliqué facedown

ART MATERIALS

See page 41.

EMBELLISHING

- 6-strand DMC embroidery floss: colors as needed for embellishment, variegated thread, and buttonhole twist
- Seed beads: colors as needed for embellishment
- Shaded wired ribbon: widths and colors as needed for Ribbon Appliqué (see Sources on page 126)
- Pipe cleaners for flower stamens in double-sided flowers

BATTING

For an antique look, use a very thin batting. The thinnest batting made today is Hobbs Thermore, a polyester material. The three thinnest cotton battings are Hobbs Heirloom Organic 100% Cotton, Organic Cotton with Scrim, and Heirloom Bleached 100% Cotton. With a pale appliqué background and a thin batting, you need a pale backing fabric so that it does not show through to the quilt top.

OPTIONAL

- Sewing light and magnification for hand work
- Thimble for appliqué and hand piecing
- Peel*n*Stick or paper-backed fusible web for making double-sided flowers (page 72)

Making
Happiness Is in the Journey
Quilt shown on page 12; Finished size: 75″ × 75″.

Notes:

- All yardages are based on 42″-wide cotton fabric.
- Ultrasuede (used in Squirrel's Berry Breakfast block, Pattern 6, page 91) is an easy option because it needs no seam allowance. It is washable; it can be ironed using the Synthetic setting; and it can be sewn with the same needle, thread, and tack stitch as cotton.
- Prewash all fabrics.
- Cut the borders lengthwise. Dogtooth borders are sized generously for ease of placement. Seam allowances are ¼″ unless noted otherwise.

MATERIALS

- Off-white background print for blocks, sashing squares, center medallion border, and first and second borders on the quilt perimeter: 5¾ yards
- Green print for sashing strips, dogtooth borders, third border on the quilt perimeter, and binding print: 4¾ yards.
  Note: This includes yardage to complete the Family History Block (Pattern 11, page 96) and foliage as needed.
- Assorted prints for the appliqué: Scraps or fat quarters in the colors of your choice. Consider using ½- to 1-yard cuts for colors that appear often.
- Batting: 83″ × 83″
- Backing: 4¾ yards

CUTTING

Off-white background print

- Cut 8 strips 10″ × width of fabric; subcut into 32 squares 10″ × 10″ for the block backgrounds; trim each to 8½″ × 8½″ after appliqué.

- Cut 1 square 20″ × 20″ for the center medallion; trim to 18″ × 18″ after appliqué.

- Cut 2 strips 3″ × width of fabric; subcut into 16 squares 3″ × 3″ for the sashing corners.

- Cut 4 strips 3½″ × 30″ for the background of the dogtooth center medallion border.

- Cut 4 strips 3½″ × 81″ for the background of the first dogtooth border on the quilt perimeter.

- Cut 4 strips 3½″ × 80″ for the second border on the quilt perimeter.

Green print

- Cut 12 strips 3″ × width of fabric; subcut into 48 rectangles 8½″ × 3″ for sashing strips.

- Cut 4 strips 2⅞″ × 30″ for the dogtooth center medallion border.

- Cut 4 strips 2⅞″ × 81″ for the first dogtooth border.

- Cut 4 strips 1½″ × 80″ for the third border.

- Cut 4 strips 2½″ × 81″ for binding.

ASSEMBLY

Refer to the quilt photo (page 12) and the Assembly Diagram (page 27) to construct the quilt top.

Quilt Blocks

The appliqué patterns for the blocks are on pages 86–110. Refer to Appliqué Basics (pages 28–70) and Pattern Transfer (pages 83–85) for instructions on making and placing the appliqué. See Appliqué a Dogtooth Border to a Block (page 40) to make the Family History Block (Pattern 11, page 96). Use the suggestions described in Art Materials and Embellishment (pages 41–82) to embellish your blocks.

1. Enlarge the center medallion pattern (page 85) 200%.

2. Prepare the 20″ × 20″ center medallion block for appliqué (see Preparing the Block Background, page 28).

3. Appliqué the block. When complete, press on the wrong side and trim to 18″ × 18″.

4. Referring to Appliqué a Dogtooth Border to a Quilt (page 40), appliqué a green dogtooth strip to a 3½″ × 30″ off-white background central medallion border strip. Repeat to make 4 dogtooth central medallion border strips.

5. Join the dogtooth borders to the center medallion block as follows. On each of the 4 finished dogtooth borders, find the bottom V between the two middle peaks of the appliquéd border, and mark it with a pin on the seamline.

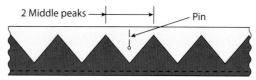

Mark center of border with pin on seamline.

6. To position the medallion borders, align the pin-marked V from Step 5 with the center medallion's vertical and horizontal centers. Pin the borders in place.

7. Stitch the borders to the edge of the medallion block, stopping ¼″ from the corner edges. Finger-press the seam allowances toward the block center.

8. Hand miter the corners by appliquéing one border on top of the adjacent border, ensuring that the dogtooth edges of the border meet at the miter. Press.

9. Trim the excess border at the miter and press. Press the border seam allowances away from the block center. Put this block aside.

10. Prepare, appliqué, and embellish the remaining 8½″ × 8½″ quilt blocks.

Quilt Assembly

Arrange the finished blocks, sashing strips, and corner squares in a pleasing arrangement in rows as shown in the Quilt Assembly Diagram (page 27).

Center Section

1. Sew a row with two 8½″ × 8½″ blocks on each side of a vertical 3″ × 8½″ sashing strip. Press the seam allowances toward the sashing strip. Repeat to make 4 rows.

2. Sew a row with two horizontal 8½″ × 3″ sashing strips on each side of a 3″ × 3″ corner square. Press the seam allowances toward the sashing strips. Repeat to make 6 rows.

3. Join 2 rows from Step 1 to 3 rows from Step 2 as shown in the Assembly Diagram. Press the seam allowances toward the horizontal sashing rows. Repeat to make 2 of these units.

4. Join a unit from Step 3 to each side of the center medallion block. Press the seam allowances away from the center.

Top and Bottom Sections

1. Sew six 8½″ × 8½″ blocks together with five 3″ × 8½″ vertical sashing strips to make a row. Press the seam allowances toward the sashing strips. Make 4 rows.

2. Sew the remaining 8½″ × 3″ horizontal sashing strips and the 3″ × 3″ corner squares together to make a row as shown. Press the seam allowances toward the sashing strips. Make 2 rows.

3. For the top section, use 2 rows from Step 1; place 1 above and 1 below a row from Step 2. Press the seam allowances toward the horizontal sashing row. Repeat to make a bottom section.

4. Sew the top section to the center section as shown. Press the seam allowances toward the center section. Similarly, join the bottom section below the center section and press.

First Dogtooth Border

1. Referring to Appliqué a Dogtooth Border to a Quilt, page 40, appliqué a green dogtooth strip to a 3½″ × 81″ off-white background border strip. Repeat to make 4 dogtooth border strips.

2. On each of the 4 finished dogtooth borders, find the middle green dogtooth peak and mark it with a pin on the seamline.

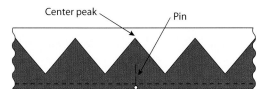
Mark center of border with pin on seamline.

3. Fold the quilt top horizontally through the center to find the center of the 2 side edges. Mark these with a pin on the seamlines. Repeat to find the center of the top and bottom edges.

4. To position a side dogtooth border, align a center pin-marked border from Step 2 with the center of the side of the quilt top. Pin the border in place. Repeat for all 4 sides.

5. To join the dogtooth borders to the quilt top, follow Steps 7–9 in Quilt Blocks (page 26).

Second and Third Borders

1. Stitch a 3½″ × 80″ off-white second border strip to the 1½″ × 80″ green third border strip along their long edges. Press toward the third border. Repeat to make 4 border strips. Press.

2. Join the borders to the quilt top, stopping ¼″ from the corner edges. Miter the corners, press, and trim excess fabric.

Finishing

Layer, quilt, and bind. Information on finishing can be found online at C&T Publishing's Quiltmaking Basics page (www.ctpub.com).

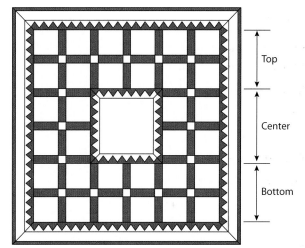
Assembly Diagram

Detail from *Happiness Is In the Journey*, Family History Block (Pattern 11, page 96), inking by Elly Sienkiewicz and appliqué by Jean F. Kearney. Dogtooth borders frame the block and the quilt.

Preparing the Block Background

Cut the block background larger than the finished size plus the seam allowances because the block may shrink during appliqué. Finger-press the block into quadrants. The pressed lines act as registration marks to help place the appliqués.

Basting

The following describes several methods of basting appliqué shapes to the background prior to stitching in place.

PIN-BASTING

Use straight pins to pin the appliqué to the background. The small, ¾″-long ball-headed pins (often called appliqué pins) work best. The ball head makes these pins easy to handle even for the very mature appliquér. Their short length prevents thread from catching on them as you stitch. Always use more than one pin so the appliqué doesn't shift or pivot. *Caution:* Even modern pins can leave rust spots over time.

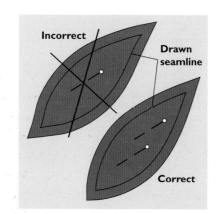

Incorrect: One pin acts as pivot.
Correct: More than one pin holds appliqué stable.

STITCH-BASTING

This is what is traditionally meant by basting: Use a milliner's needle [a], nonslippery thread, and medium-length (⅛″–¼″) running stitches [b]. Use appliqué pins [c] to hold each piece in place while you baste. Begin with a knot [d].

Secure the stitches before ending and remove the stitches after you have appliquéd with finer stitches.

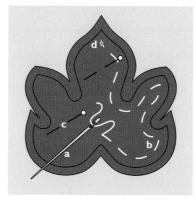

Stitch-basting

GLUE-BASTING WITH A GLUESTICK

I avoid putting gluestick on the wrong side of the finished appliqué because I am concerned about migration or staining. Instead I apply the glue on the seam allowance or on a freezer-paper template (to be used inside the appliqué) that will be removed. Gluestick has an advantage over the liquid white glue in that it adheres immediately.

Freezer paper, shiny side up

Gluestick dabbed on the exposed seam

Dab gluestick along back of exposed seam allowance. Gluestick on seam allowance is pressed to background fabric.

Finger-press appliqué in place, and it's ready to stitch.

To attach fabric to fabric: Use a glue-stick to apply a dab of glue to hold the point in the Freezer Paper Inside technique (at right).

To attach freezer paper to fabric: In appliqués prepared with Freezer Paper Inside, dab gluestick on the exposed back of the freezer paper to baste the appliqué to the background fabric.

NOTE

You can use gluestick instead of an iron to hold the turned-under seam allowance to the paper (see Prepared Appliqué with Freezer Paper Inside, at right).

The secret is that the shiny side of the paper will hold the glued fabric long enough to do the appliqué. But twisting the paper/fabric adhesion breaks the seal, allowing the paper to be easily removed from inside the appliqué.

HEAT-BASTING

Use the tip of a hot iron to meld freezer paper to the wrong side of fabric in pin-basting-like intervals. Heat baste to smoothly fold fabric into a curved edge. Or heat baste an appliqué to the background fabric using the Freezer Paper Inside technique (page 29). The still-exposed shiny side of the freezer paper beneath the appliqué makes this possible. Set the iron to Cotton. A too-hot iron setting, such as Linen, may scorch the background fabric.

The Tack Stitch

Although the blanket, running, ladder, or blind stitch can be used for appliqué, the only one you really need to know is the tack stitch. Here, though, let's celebrate the tack stitch and refine it. The tack stitch holds all three layers—background, seam allowance, and appliqué—but shows only a tiny bit (the width of one needle) at the turn line.

1. Begin the tack stitch by pushing the needle up from underneath the background to emerge a full needle-width inside the fold of the appliqué [a]. When the needle emerges, pull the thread away from yourself until it is stopped by the knot on the back [b].

Push needle up from back. Pull thread away.

2. Reinsert the point of the needle under the fold, as though you were putting it back into the same hole from which it emerged. The thread should not pull forward on the diagonal like a whipstitch, nor should it pull backward on the diagonal like a backstitch. What Goldilocks would call "just right" is a tiny, straight, perpendicular stitch one needle-width from the fold of the turned-under appliqué and then wrapping around the fold.

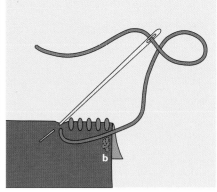

Reinsert needle.

3. To complete the stitch, exit the background fabric, scraping your finger beneath the block to make sure you're all the way through. All in one motion, turn the needle sharply upward again. Pierce up through the background, through the seam allowance, and through the appliqué, catching it just to the left of the previous stitch. Continue with about 10 stitches per inch. There is no correct number of stitches per inch. The test is: Does the appliqué look good from the top, and does it hold well?

Prepared Appliqué with Freezer Paper Inside

There are two major appliqué families: the Prepared Appliqué family and the Nonprepared Appliqué family (starting on page 32). Of all the many ways to prepare appliqué, my favorite is to preturn and hold under the seam allowance using Freezer Paper Inside. This technique is often used for Separate Unit Appliqué when individual units are added to an appliqué block. With the following technique, you *iron* the seam allowance to the shiny side of the freezer paper.

POINTS, CURVES, AND STRAIGHT EDGES

Let this leaf and heart motif show you how to prepare (to preturn under) the seam allowance at outside corners, inside corners, straight edges, and curves using Freezer Paper Inside.

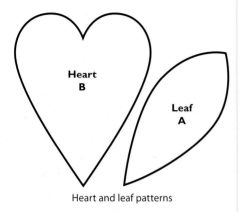

Heart and leaf patterns

Points

1. Trace the leaf shape (Pattern A) onto freezer paper. Cut directly on the drawn line (adding no seam allowance). Pin it shiny side up to the wrong side of the appliqué fabric, on the bias where possible.

2. Cut out the leaf with a ³⁄₁₆″ seam allowance beyond the freezer paper.

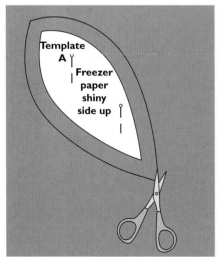

Pin freezer-paper template shiny side up on wrong side of fabric. Cut out with ³⁄₁₆″ seam allowance.

3. Pin the point of the freezer paper to a cardboard work surface so that it does not fold back as you iron [a]. Iron the seam allowance point perpendicular to the leaf [b].

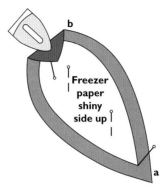

Pin point and iron seam allowance.

4. Smear gluestick across the width of the point. Finger-press the left side and then the right side into the glue so that the point is prepared (that is, it is all turned under). Heat press the point once more to dry the glue. On an ovate leaf, do one point, and then the other.

Finger-press sides of point into glue, press, and prepare other point.

Curves and Straight Edges

Curves or straight edges? Heat baste (page 29) the seam allowance with the point of the iron [a], spacing the intervals to keep the fabric turning in the desired direction. Finish the appliqué preparation by using a smoothing motion [b] with the side of the iron (like frosting a cake) to smoothly turn

under the heat-basted sides. Remove the pins. From the front side, the appliqué should look finished.

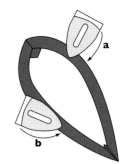

Fold sides of curves and straight edges, and press.

OUTSIDE AND INSIDE CORNERS

1. Turn the outside point of a heart [d] first, as you did for the leaf.

2. For the inside corner, cut, dividing the seam allowance equally between the shoulders of the heart, stopping 3 needle-widths short of the paper [e]. *Hint:* Never clip right to the paper when using a freezer-paper template. If you think your clip has gone too far, clip the paper itself to allow a deeper stitch into the fabric corner.

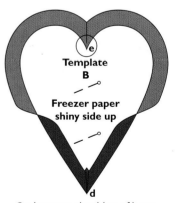

Cut between shoulders of heart.

3. Fold down half of the V-cut so that you can more easily access the opposite side.

Fold shoulder down to make preparing inside corner easier.

4. When you've ironed one side, open it, then repeat the folding and ironing process for the opposite side.

Repeat on other side of heart.

5. When the heart is fully prepared over paper, pin or baste (page 28) it to the background, and appliqué it down.

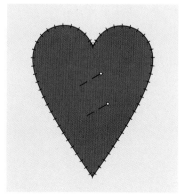

Appliqué prepared heart to background.

REMOVING FREEZER-PAPER TEMPLATES

When you have finished all the stitching, remove the template by slitting the background fabric beneath the appliqué. Stop the cut ¼″ short of the appliquéd seamline. Pinch the seam between your thumb and forefinger to hold it steady and avoid stretching the stitches. Reach into the slit with tweezers or a hemostat and remove the freezer paper. Alternatively, you can leave an opening in the appliqué and remove the paper from the front, then complete the appliqué.

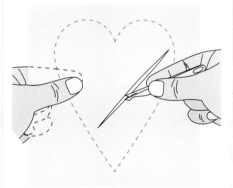

Remove freezer paper after appliqué is complete.

Separate Unit Appliqué with Freezer Paper Inside

Pattern 17, the Grapevine Lyre Wreath (page 102), is a good example of when to use Separate Unit Appliqué. The vine stem is first appliquéd in place, and then other leaf shapes are prepared using Freezer Paper Inside. These are then appliquéd on top of the stems, as a second layer (top) of appliqué. See Prepared Appliqué with Freezer Paper Inside (pages 29–31) to prepare these shapes, and then appliqué them in place using the tack stitch (page 29).

LAYERED APPLIQUÉ
Overlap and Underlap

Second or top shapes can be made as separate fabric units with the freezer-paper template inside and can be appliquéd over the top of a first shape (first shape appliquéd directly on the background fabric), covering the exposed seam allowance. This type of appliqué is called *layering*. This is done by placing an appliqué motif over or under another motif. Common sense tells us when and how to do it. There is no magic to Layered Appliqué. Simply analyze the pattern and judge which layer goes down first. As far as what looks best, the following customary layering sequences come to mind:

- Leaves go over stems.
- Buds go under calyxes.
- Necks go under collars; heads go over necks.

You get the picture!

NOTE

A seam that gets turned under, over another seam, is called an **overlap**. A seam that lies flat (unturned) under another layer's turned seam is called an **underlap**. Cut the underlap a full ¼″ wide so it is simpler to cover when the next layer is turned above it. Underlaps are used to reduce bulk under appliquéd shapes within the block. For example, in Pattern 4, Crossed Stems with Yo-Yo Roses, (*page 89*), the ends of the rose stems lie flat under the flowers; there is no need to turn the ends under.

Nonprepared Appliqué

NEEDLETURN APPLIQUÉ

Needleturn is the most familiar form of Nonprepared Appliqué. The seams are not turned under ahead of time; rather, the needle turns under the seam allowance during the appliqué. Needleturn can also be used for Separate Unit Appliqué (page 31). You can draw the pattern on the appliqué fabric, in which case the drawn line is the turn line.

You can also use Needleturn for connected appliqué shapes. In Baltimores, the most common connected appliqué patterns are papercuts, which are used in Patterns 1 through 13 (pages 86–98). The ideal way to appliqué papercuts is to use Needleturn Appliqué combined with Cutaway Appliqué.

CUTAWAY APPLIQUÉ

In Cutaway Appliqué, the appliqué is cut out—not all at once, but an inch or two at a time—then needleturned under. The advantages are that the uncut fabric keeps the appliqué from shifting and fraying. Cutaway allows you to avoid time-consuming basting and to appliqué sooner. The beauty of this method is in its simplicity. Following are its two short rules.

Rule 1: Never cut around a point. Always cut a generous inch past the point whenever possible [a]. Continue that cut in the same direction as the seam.

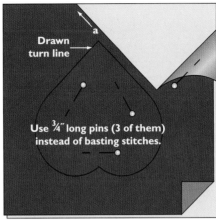

Drawn turn line

Use ¾″ long pins (3 of them) instead of basting stitches.

Always cut beyond point.

Rule 2: Never change the direction of your cut until you stitch the first side of a point (or corner) [b].

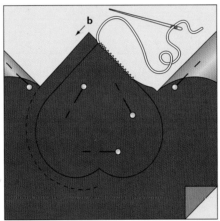

Don't change direction of cut until after point or corner is stitched.

Preparing a Block for Cutaway Appliqué

1. Cut 1 square 9″ × 9″ of background fabric and carefully fold it into quarters, right side out [a]. Do the same for 1 square 9″ × 9″ of appliqué fabric [b]. The crease lines act as registration marks.

2. Transfer the pattern to the appliqué fabric (page 83).

3. Layer the marked appliqué square (right side up) on top of the background square (also right side up).

4. Pin the layers together in the 4 corners and in the center. Pin from the back [c] to avoid catching the thread as you sew.

5. Put 3 small appliqué pins (from the front [d]) in the area where you'll begin to appliqué. These pins should be moved ahead as you sew, for they are always securing the area you're sewing. Check the back periodically to ensure that the layers are lying flat.

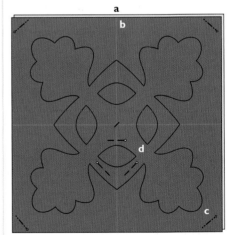

Prepare block for Cutaway Appliqué.

POINTS, CURVES, AND CORNERS

Needleturn rewards practice. It takes skill to turn a fine point, to sweep under a corner, or to stitch a curved seam—but once learned, it gives great joy. In Prepared Appliqué, where the seam-turning has been done beforehand, the stitching is always the same. In contrast, Needleturn Appliqué requires unique techniques for tucking under outside points, creating clean inside corners, and molding rounded curves. Let's learn the secrets of Needleturn Appliqué. We'll use an Oak Leaf and Reel Pattern to illustrate the basics.

Outside Points

We all like a challenge, and every outside point poses one. Happily, a wonderful formula for turning a perfect point exists. And it works! The illustration shows no freezer-paper template, just a drawn turn line. It also shows a right-hander stitching—all right-handers approach points from the right, whereas left-handers approach from the left.

Perfect Point Preparation

▦ Take close, fine stitches (one needle-width from the fold) for the last ¼″ before the point [a].

▦ Take the last stitch right into the drawn turn line itself [b].

▦ If the lower seam allowance sticks out like a dog-ear [c], clip it off.

▦ Pull the background fabric firmly over your forefinger beneath the block. This holds the background still as you move the appliqué seams under the corner.

Prepare for perfect point.

Formula for a Perfect Point

Step 1: PUSH

The push takes control of the exposed seam allowances on the point, the ones you want tucked smoothly beneath the point. Always push close to the raw edge and close to the fold, never in the midseam allowance.

A. The Basic Push (my favorite): Push using a round toothpick or the tips of your embroidery scissors. With the sharp tip, push down hard (close to the fold; close to the raw edge [f]) against the seam so the top and bottom seam allowances pivot under as one. This technique gives you greater control for very sharp points and frayed or otherwise difficult points.

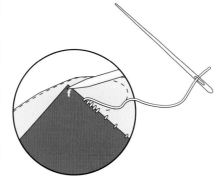

Basic Push: Use round wooden toothpick or tip of fine embroidery scissors.

B. The Needle Push: Same as A, but use the point of your sewing needle. This technique works for modest points.

C. The Woven Push: Weave the needle in and out of the folded-under seam allowance [e], but not into the background. You'll need a full ³⁄₁₆″-wide seam allowance to get enough of a bite to work.

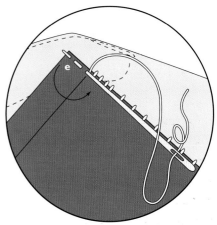

Use needle for Woven Push.

Step 2: PIVOT

Push down and around, jamming the seam fold to a stop against the sewn seam [g]. Do this with such assurance that the last stitches are loosened [h]. The motion of the pivot is that of making a hospital corner with a bedsheet.

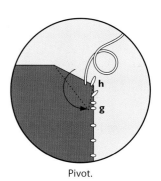

Pivot.

Step 3: PINCH

Completely cover the turned point with your thumb. Because you previously pushed so assertively down and to the right, you can now push, with your thumb pinched to your forefinger, up to the left.

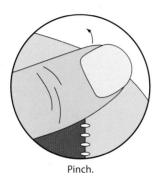

Pinch.

Step 4: PULL

Remove your thumb. If you did everything right, your point will look terribly wrong. The last stitches taken will have been pulled loose. Pull the hanging thread [i]. The fold should magically slip out into a finely turned point.

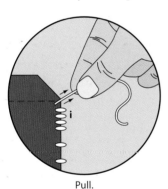

Pull.

Step 5: POINT TO THE POINT

If you've turned the point neatly, you can choose to lock it in place with this stitch: Pierce the background 2 threads beyond the point [1], bringing the needle up through the point at [2] and continue stitching. *Note:* Make sure the descent stitches [j] mirror the ascent.

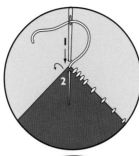

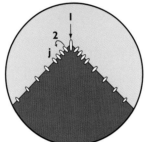

Point to the point.

Elongate the Point

The magical lazy daisy stitch elongates the point.

1. When you get to the stitch at the point, pull the thread to the left and hold it there with your left thumb.

2. Center your needle so it is pointing upward and push it into the appliqué point at [1] to emerge 2 background threads beyond the point at [2], passing over the looped thread [a].

Pass point of needle over looped thread.

3. Pause and use the point of your closed embroidery scissors (or a toothpick) to tuck under the left seam allowance of the point for about ½″ or so [b]. When the slope from the point looks correct, finger-press to crease the seam.

4. Resume by pulling the needle and thread just taut [3], then pierce the background at [4], forming a lazy daisy stitch.

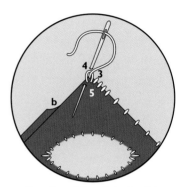

Form lazy daisy stitch at point.

5. Bring the needle up at [5] to begin the first downhill stitch. Make these first downhill stitches mirror the uphill ones in fineness and closeness [c]. *Note:* If done just right, the embroidered lazy daisy stitch gives the impression of a sharper point, especially when done in a 50- or 60-weight thread in the same color as the appliqué.

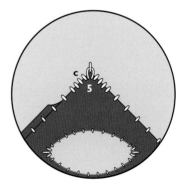

Make descending stitches match ascending stitches.

Outward Curves

Unlike patchwork, appliqué positively rollicks with curves. Once an appli-quér turns her thoughts to finely sewn curves, she likely will produce them. Why? Because bumps on a curve do not pop up behind what you've just stitched. Bumps on a curve are folds created *before* you sew them in. (If this feels like a guilt trip, fear not: You can avoid it.) Just work out those bumps *before* you sew. Think of the outward curve as a hill that you'll traverse in three stages: climbing, cresting, and descending. Trying to deal with the whole hill all at once actually leads to peaks in the curve. In Needleturn Appliqué, your thumb holds the part of the curve you've just needleturned

under. *The secret on a curve is to stop stitching ⅛″ in front of your thumb so that you can change the direction in which the seam allowance lies beneath the appliqué.*

For alluring curves, try this:

1. Cut a narrower (⅛″) seam allowance on an outside curve [a]. This gives less bulk to turn under.

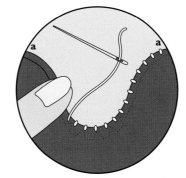

Cut narrower seam allowance on outside curves.

2. With the point of the needle, catch the seam and pull it under toward you, sweeping your needle from left to right [b] with regal authority—self-confidence helps! Pinch and hold the turned seam to finger-press it.

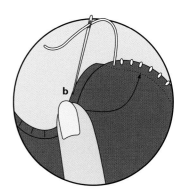

Sweep under seam.

POINTERS FOR MAKING POINTIER POINTS

The formula for a perfect point is push, pivot, pinch, pull, and point to the point for … a *perfect point!*

Follow these hints for supersharp points, but use caution:

■ To reduce the bulk, cut out a wedge from the bottom seam allowance [a] (the seam that has already been sewn).

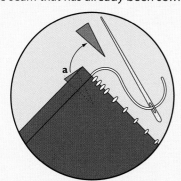

Cut wedge from seam allowance.

■ To reduce the bulk, cut the seam allowance just ⅛″ wide [b].

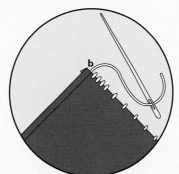

Use ⅛″ seam allowance.

First Aid for Fray

If you have not had much experience and want to try these risky points, paint the seam cutting line [d] with clear nail polish [c] to seal the threads. Let it dry, then cut the ⅛″-wide finer seam by cutting through the center of the sealed area [e]. Unlike commercial fabric fray sealers, nail polish does not bleed easily; but be careful not to paint close to the turn line itself.

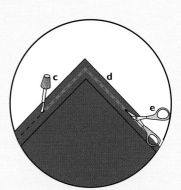

Use nail polish as first aid for fray.

3. Tackstitch (page 29) to within ⅛″ of your thumb [c]. Stop and lift your thumb so that you can use the point of the needle to catch the turned-under seam allowance [d]. With a windshield wiper–like motion, change the direction of the folds to lie flat. Pinch the curve. Each time you move farther left, work the seam allowance so that the folds follow the changing curve. Follow that curve, one steady stitch at a time.

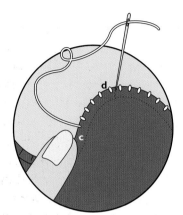

Work needle beneath seam allowance to make folds lie flat.

4. If your curve inadvertently peaks, return to the culprit even after the stitching is finished [d, again]. Slip the needle under the seam, use that same windshield wiper–like motion to snag the underneath seam on the point of the needle, and pull the seam allowance smooth. Then finger-press it to flat perfection.

Inside Curves

Use a normal ³⁄₁₆″- to ⅛″-deep seam allowance on an inside curve. The general rule is to clip the seam allowance. Cut every ¼″ or so, perpendicular to the deepest part of the curve. When the curve is marked with a drawn line, clip to 2 needle-widths short of the drawn line. When a freezer-paper template marks the pattern, clip ⅔ of the seam allowance. Think of the ¼″ of fabric

between clips as a tab [a]. Use the point of the needle to catch the tab and pull it toward you beneath the appliqué. Never place the shank of the needle right in the clip. The object is to turn past the clip so that the clip is swept smoothly under. Start at the top of the curve [b], sweeping under the seam allowance and following close upon that sweep to cover and crease the turn line with your left thumb.

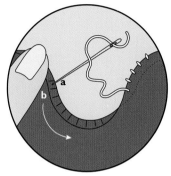

Needleturn inside curves.

Right-Angle Inside Corners

Inside corners are fascinating. In my experience, inside corners fit roughly into three main types: Vs, U-turns, and some combination of the two. Each has its customized appliqué approach. The prototype V corner is the right-angle corner. Here's how to tackle such a corner.

1. Stop appliquéing ½″ before the corner [a]. Cut into, but not beyond, the corner's turn line [b]. When the corner is symmetrical, as shown, cut to divide the seam allowance in half equally, from one side to the other. *Note:* Remember that when using a freezer-paper template (instead of a drawn line, as shown here), the freezer paper guides the appliqué and the turn line is ¹⁄₁₆″ beyond the edge of the paper. So here, the corner clip [b] would be ¹⁄₁₆″ above the ironed-on freezer-paper template.

2. Rest three-quarters of the needle over the seam allowance flap, with the front quarter [c] moving freely between the appliqué fabric and the background. This way, your needle is positioned to catch and cleanly sweep under that flap.

3. Place your thumb squarely over the corner so that by pressing thumb to forefinger [d], you can pinch-crease the seam as you sweep it under.

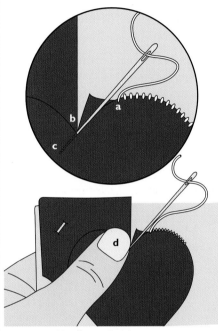

Needleturn inside corner.

4. Lighten your pinch to withdraw the needle and then resume the pressure. Tackstitch up to your thumb. Nothing different happens [e] until the last stitch before the inside corner [1]. *Note:* The last stitch before an inward corner is begun 3 needle-widths into the appliqué and finishes entering the background under the fold of the seam directly opposite where it began.

Continued on page 38

CURING THE IMPOSSIBLY NARROW INSIDE CORNER

One option is to clip into the corner, short of the turn line. This makes the angle less acute and widens the seam allowance. *Note:* To change the angle, the turn line marking must be impermanent. As an example, use a freezer-paper template to mark the turn line of the original pattern [a]. Then use a silver-colored pencil to trace the outline of the template, lifting the inward point [b] to give enough seam allowance to safely turn the inward point. Notice that the dashed cutting line [c] also shows a narrower seam allowance over the shoulder curve of the heart [d] and a wider seam allowance at the inside corner [e]. Cut into the drawn line [f] and turn under [g] this wider seam allowance. This helps the turned fabric stay under. You are the captain of the appliqué ship—on any pattern, your way is the right way.

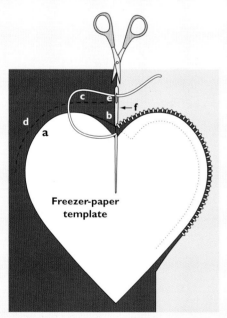

Change angle of corner.

Paint the cutting line with clear nail polish [h]. When the V is dry, divide it with a cut [i] into, but not beyond, the turn line [j]. With this technique, the tiny seam allowance turns under more safely and easily, as long as you have not stiffened the turn line with the polish!

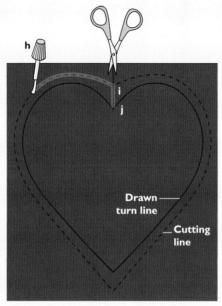

Drawn turn line

Cutting line

Use nail polish on cutting line.

The Gluestick Trick: When a fabric frays easily, or with any challenging corner, draw your needle over an open gluestick [k]. When you sweep under the seam allowance [l], the glue comes off onto the seam allowance. Once turned under, the seam allowance will adhere [m] to the background fabric, acting like a third hand and holding it in place while you proceed to stitch under the seam. If you are concerned about a gummed-up needle, pinch the appliqué to the background to clean off the glue as you withdraw the needle.

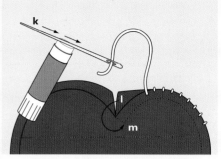

Use the Gluestick Trick.

Use the lazy daisy way with corner fray. When a thread that is as long as the seam allowance is wide [n] separates from the left seam allowance, consider it a "good fray." Because the thread is long, it will stay tucked in after you push it back under. A short fray [o] is more worrisome. After you tuck it under, it might pop out again. Take a lazy daisy stitch (page 34) to secure the inside point [p]. The lazy daisy leaves 3 threads that act like a dike [q] to hold back any fuzzies.

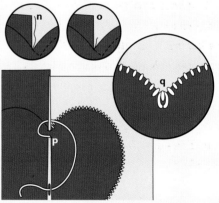

Handle frays

5. The stitch at the inward corner begins by coming up 4 needle-widths into the appliqué and finishes going under the seam's fold (but not into the background), coming up through the appliqué fabric again at [2]. It is taken twice [3], making a loop that—pulled taut—rolls the raw edge under.

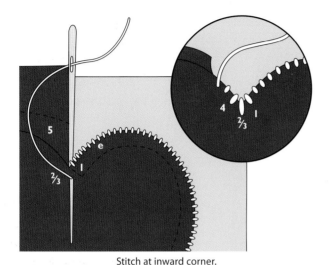

Stitch at inward corner.

6. Cut 1½″ along the dotted line, then needleturn the left side, beginning ½″ to the left of the inward point [5]. Complete the corner with a stitch 3 needle-widths deeper [4].

Inside Corners

Raindrop Corners

Some appliqué corners are all curves, like raindrops or U-turns. Of course, we'll master these, too!

1. When your stitches reach ½″ [a] from the bottom, clip the deepest part of the curve in the shape of a crow's foot [b]. Cut just short of, but not into, the drawn line [c].

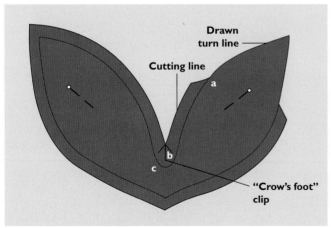

Needleturn U-turn corner.

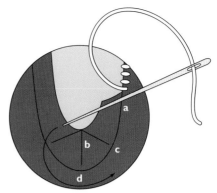

Clip just short of drawn line.

2. Begin above the farthest clip, catching the seam with the tip of the needle and pulling it down and around [d], under the appliqué. Quick as a wink, follow the needle with your thumb, finger-pressing the crease between your thumb and forefinger [e].

3. Continue to finger-press as you stitch toward your thumb, taking a series of normally spaced but deeper (2 needle-widths) stitches [f]. Give a slight tug as you pull each stitch through—you're pulling the fold under, as though you were rolling under the edge of a silk scarf. Midway around the raindrop curve, you may need to repeat Step 2 to keep the seam turned under.

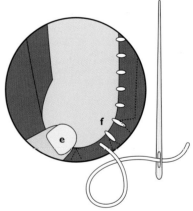

Finger-press and stitch around curve.

Leaf/Stem Corners

A leaf and stem can be cut from one piece of fabric. This simplified construction so appealed to me that I made it the basic technique for stitching the majority of the lessons in my previous books. Now, almost two decades later, this technique is more common in our contemporary Albums than in the old Baltimores!

1. Stop when your stitches are ½″ away [a] and cut into the corner turn line at a 45° angle [b].

2. Place the needle in the corner flap. Pinch it between your thumb and forefinger and sweep it down and around [c].

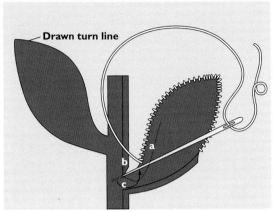

Curved corner meets straight stem.

3. Take a series of slightly deeper (2 needle-widths) stitches until the last stitch before the corner.

4. At the corner, take the deeper (2 needle-widths) stitch directly opposite the slash. Take this stitch twice so that it loops over the edge. Pull it taut so that it rolls the corner under [d].

5. Finish the stem side of the corner with one more slightly longer stitch [e].

Finished leaf/stem corner

PATTERN BRIDGES

Sometimes you must add pattern bridges to get the benefit of unit cutwork. Temporarily leaving the center of a cutwork pattern in place or creating a small link between two sides of a pattern is called creating a *pattern bridge* (see Pattern 1, Roses for Hans Christian Andersen, page 86). These disposable bridges keep a fragile pattern from being ironed on crookedly to the appliqué fabric. Once the pattern is positioned, carefully snip the dotted bridge lines and pull out the pattern bridge, which has now served its purpose.

Block Completion

PRESS THE APPLIQUÉ

Place the block, appliqué side down, on a worn terry-cloth towel. Use an inexpensive (not deeply embossed) paper towel as a pressing cloth. Place it over the wrong side of the block. Lightly spray the paper towel with Magic Sizing spray finish. Magic Sizing inhibits bleeding when you inscribe fabric. Years ago, to my dismay, the cotton appliqué thread bled. To my relief, it bled up into the paper towel, making me a believer in paper towel pressing cloths.

TRIM THE BLOCK TO SIZE

Place your finished block right side down on a flat surface. Center the 8½″ × 8½″ square gridded ruler or plastic template (page 24) over the block. Draw the cutting line around the template. Cut out the square. For machine piecing, the presser foot is a sufficient guide for stitching the ¼″ seam. For hand piecing, you can draw a sewing line ¼″ inside the cut edge using a gridded ruler.

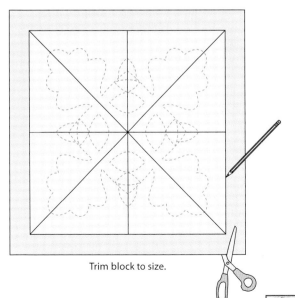

Trim block to size.

Dogtooth Borders: Antique Template-Free Appliqué

In our *Happiness Is in the Journey* quilt (page 12), the Family History Block (Pattern 11), center medallion block (Pattern 25), and the first inner border of the quilt all have dogtooth borders, or strings of triangles—a common Baltimore Album border. You could practice your Needleturn Appliqué for this border. But before you consider that, read on about dogtooth borders. If you practice them, they will dance in your imagination and become a dramatic, easy solution for bordering your quilt. When using the template-free method of dogtooth borders, rather than cutting the normal seam allowance up to the points and down to the valleys, you will tuck under the entire triangular seam allowance. To practice the folding, cut a 2½" × 11" strip of paper; when doing so, consider how easily you can size and appliqué this sort of border!

APPLIQUÉ A DOGTOOTH BORDER TO A BLOCK

To apply this technique to the Family History Block:

1. Pin the block below the "border" 3 to 5 times.

2. Imagine that each triangle has a number, from 1 at the right corner to 10 at the left. Draw a straight line [a] parallel to and ⅛" above the points of triangles 1–10 and trim it off. Cut into each drawn inside point on the grain, splitting the seam allowance equally between the adjacent triangles [b].

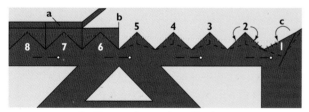

Prepare dogtooth appliqué.

3. Fold under the left side of Triangle 1. Use the shank of your needle to turn under the triangle as you would any angular corner. Then begin the appliqué in the middle of that seam [c].

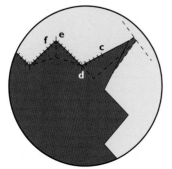

Begin in middle of seam.

4. When you reach the bottom of the valley, take your slightly long stitch, then take the longer stitch of the inside corner twice (page 30). Needleturn under the right side of the next triangle to finish the inside point [d], taking close stitches just before the outside point [e], turning the point [f], and so on.

5. The corner point seam is bulkier than the side triangles. Open the seam and clip out the excess as needed.

6. Once you've turned the point of Triangle 1, you've finished the appliqué. Congratulations!

APPLIQUÉ A DOGTOOTH BORDER TO A QUILT

1. Pin the strip of fabric for the dogtooth border to the length of the background fabric for that border.

2. For *Happiness Is in the Journey*, without using a template, mark off the dogtooth strip at equal intervals of 1½". Mark only about 10" at a time. At every other mark, put a dot ⅛" from the top edge for the seam allowance [a].

3. At the marks in between, cut down 2" on the grain line. Adjust the width of the marks and the depth of the cuts to size the dogteeth as desired if you are making a different sized quilt.

4. Beginning at the right end, fold under the left side of the first triangle, then fold under the right side of the next triangle. Begin appliquéing in the middle of the first fold and stitch to the base of the triangle. Appliqué up the right side of the adjacent triangle, stopping ⅛" from the top. Continue in this manner across the strip.

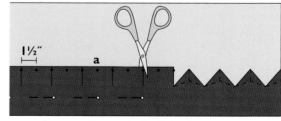

Prepare dogtooth border.

ART MATERIALS AND EMBELLISHMENT

Unique antique clipper ship: Ombréd fabric affects the look of dimension while skillful pen-work rigs and spars the sails. The crew is on deck, and the ship is full of architectural details. Also revealed are the cannons, which are typically shuttered by *trompe d'oeil* windows. Colorful high-flying flags frame half the ship, but no familiar floral garland frames the sea. Note how lushly the artist inked the "moss" of the rosebuds moss (block fragment to right). *Photo courtesy Jeanne Glenfield*

Why Art Materials?

How is the term *art materials* used here? Not definitively, but to include traditional one-dimensional art materials such as paints, inks, and pastels; and vintage three-dimensional fancywork techniques, such as fabric manipulations that include folding, gathering, and weaving. Our art materials are rich with goods of the world: embroidery threads, traditional and innovative in cottons, silks, wool, and synthetics; beads, antique and modern; and a wealth of however briefly accessible couturiere ribbons. Art materials, so accessible in our day, are beautifully apparent in the pictured works of our contemporary needleartist contributors.

FASCINATION TURNED TO LOVE

An antique appliqué, pictured in a book, perplexed me. The urn's fabric undulated with depths and highlights as though watercolored. How had this look been achieved? By painting on velvet, perhaps? It was 1981 and the Baltimore Museum of Art advertised an exhibition of antebellum Baltimore Album Quilts—just the sort of quilt where that urn block had been

appliquéd. I drove to Baltimore. The exhibit I lingered over there changed my life. I discovered that mysterious shaded look was a rollerprint textile style of the era. I felt awe at the intricate appliqués. I sensed the quiltmakers' presence. In autumn of 1982, I brought my first Baltimore appliqué book to Quilt Market in Houston: *Spoken Without a Word—A Lexicon of Selected Symbols with 24 Patterns from Classic Baltimore Album Quilts.*

Baltimore Beauties and Beyond, Volume One, my first lesson and pattern book, was published in 1989. Multiple Baltimore Album Quilt (BAQ) books were out by the mid-1990s. Baltimores had become a quilt force across the industrialized world. Carter Houck, *Quilter's Circle* editor, dubbed it the "Baltimore Album Revival," and it continues today. The revival had renewed manufacture of the mid-nineteenth century's ombréd fabric, but like Civil War reenactors rolling their own cigarettes for authenticity, Baltimore aficionadas began exploring art materials and re-creating Baltimore's classic watercolored look for themselves. Thus they echo Baltimore artists of yesteryear, who painted cheeks on doves, faces on figures, and colorwash to penned images like the Queen of the May (pictured on the jacket of *Baltimore Beauties and Beyond, Volume Two*).

THE PRINCIPLES OF DESIGN

Serendipitously, new primary evidence surfaced last year on Album attributions: Dr. Seiss's published 1856 graduation address to the well-established Women's Division of the School of Design of the Maryland Institute. Founded in Baltimore in 1826, the institute today is America's oldest art college. Women of the Album era attended the institute to learn "Principles of Design." Recognizing excellence, Dr. W. R. Dunton, in *Old Quilts* (1948), asks, "Who could have been the artist behind these exceptional quilts?" The institute held annual fairs from 1848 to 1856 at which Albums were hung. Quiltmakers' names were published in show catalogs, and the winners were published in *The Baltimore Sun* newspaper. Ronda McAllen, checking recent Baltimore Album artist attributions to Mary Evans and

Baltimore Clipper Ship (Pattern 25, page 110) from the antique, interpreted by Evelyn Crovo Hall. Art material embellishment includes heavy Sakura Specialist Oil Pastel edge shading of the grayed batik sails. The roses are carefully cut using a window template (page 65). The same darkened rose edge would result from stencil shading (page 48) the red with dark purple oil pastel.

The garland embroidery is remarkable! Leaf veins and margins are embroidered, moss or fern is built on a central stem stitch branched with lazy daisy stitches, bead embroidered at the branch's crotch. See pages 112, and 115 for detail embroidery and flag-making techniques. *Photo by Evelyn Crovo Hall*

Mary Simon, combed the institute catalog and *Sun* newspaper databases but found neither Mary. Nor has other evidence sufficiently supported their authorship. Indeed, was Dr. Dunton on the right path in seeking a dominant "artist"?

Might the institute itself be the elephant in the room of Album attribution? Even today, one humble quiltmaker's clever design innovation transmits through classes, shows, publications, and more to spread through the quilt world anonymously, like sweet perfume over a theater crowd. Would not an active Women's Division in the Institute of Design have inevitably influenced the artistry of this small city's quiltmaking subcultures? There had to have been links: Institute board member surnames (men's names, perhaps as a form of philanthropy) appear randomly inscribed on certain Baltimore blocks. Perhaps from you, Dear Reader, we can hope for more research—perhaps a starting date for the Women's Division, for example.

GOD, FREE TRADE, AND THE BALTIMORES

Dr. Seiss, in his address, made an emotional appeal for financial support to the Women's Design Division. He pled the need for young women to study the principles of design for their good and the nation's. Millions of dollars, he argued,

drained annually to Europe for textiles of no better quality than America's but with more marketable design. Empathetically he decried these women's prospects in Baltimore of 1856: The seemingly ceaseless drain of men to the West left women behind with little hope of marriage and few skills for honest employ. Seiss orated with passionate sincerity on the morally uplifting effects of art study (all beauty being a self-revealing gift from God). He observed that art studies would benefit the nation's budding textile industry internationally, even as it benefited the souls and economic needs of Baltimore's young women.

CAN THE USE OF PRINCIPLES OF DESIGN BE SEEN?

Typically, nineteenth-century clipper ship paintings depict dark sea, pale sky, black hull, whitish sails, and astern, a flag. Without the benefit of framing, such a depiction wouldn't meld particularly well if set among Album blocks. Might flags atop the clouds of sail and a floating garland beneath the sea witness an evolving design principle for framing clipper ships? Like the differing renditions of rosebuds in calyxes—so many clever depictions that they might have been an art class assignment—the Albums are full of exploration and innovation within this Album style. Let's honor our Baltimore sisters' industrious ingenuity in developing fresh, possibly marketable design: Let us consider those art materials (ink, pens, oil pastels, paint, ribbons, embroidery threads, and beads) used with increasing innovation in today's Album Quilts.

Acrylic Paint and Ink Supplies

We'll start our art material appliqué with painting, for that is the newest technique for me—this even though there are painted details in the antique Baltimores. Rare, these painted details are in the fanciest-style blocks, but their presence emphasizes the Baltimorean sense of these quilts as fine art. As we start the fourth decade of the Baltimore Album revival, it seems appropriate to finally pick up our brushes as did our sisters of yore. Techniques for art materials on fabric follow with exercises to teach yourself and others.

BASIC SUPPLIES

Paint and Inks

Available at your local quilt or art store or from C&T Publishing; I used the following materials:

- Winsor & Newton Special Value Golden Synthetic Brush Pack or other basic brushes
- Liquitex Soft Body Acrylic Colors (high pigment content; brilliant colors; creamy smooth flow; excellent for both coverage and fine, fine detail, dries flexible) in Cadmium Red Medium, Titanium White, Hookers Green Hue, Phthalocyanine Green, Ultramarine Blue, Bright Aqua Green, Burnt Sienna, Raw Sienna, Cadmium Yellow Medium, and Phthalocyanine Blue
- Liquitex Professional Acrylic Ink! (smooth fluid consistency; clear colors; even flow; dries quickly to permanent, water-resistant finish; comes capped with convenient eye-dropper dispenser) in Napthol Crimson, Yellow Medium Azo, and Phthalocyanine Green

Other Supplies

Available from art and/or craft stores

- Small inexpensive paint-mixing tray
- Dip pen with several medium to fine points
- Size 0 round brush for finest detail painting
- Pigma pens .01 and .05 in black
- Fine-lead mechanical pencil for tracing onto fabric stabilized with Magic Sizing or freezer paper
- Cut-to-the-point 5″ fabric scissors and paper scissors

Fabric

- 1 yard high-thread-count muslin or white sheeting, torn into fat quarters
- Light to medium shades of tone-on-tone prints
- Light to medium shades of solids for specific overdyed painting effects

FABRIC PREPARATION

Preshrink your fabric before painting for appliqué. Why? Because the appliqué templates by which shapes will be drawn and cut from this cloth are actual size with no allowance for shrinkage. Preshrink by bringing the fabric to a boil in a microwave and ironing it dry or by ironing any soaked cloth until dry.

Has color come out in the rinse/wash water? This is *loose dye*. Although it has colored the water, I find it does not bleed into surrounding cloth when well washed as an appliqué. Nonetheless, wash the preshrunk hand-painted cloth with liquid hand soap or Ivory, rinse, and repeat if necessary until all loose dye is out. Then heat set by ironing.

Painting Techniques

Dry cloth? Wet cloth? The following is an introduction to two major approaches to painted appliqué.

APPROACH 1: STARTING WITH DRY FABRIC

With this method you draw, then paint specific objects on dry fabric to be cut out and appliquéd.

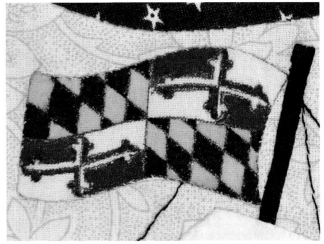

Maryland flag atop a clipper ship by Tina Cole. Painted using Approach 1 and appliquéd (complete clipper ship block on page 48).

Photo by Matthew Cole

EXERCISE: PAINT A FLAG TO APPLIQUÉ

1. Stabilize prewashed (preshrunk) white fabric by ironing freezer paper to the wrong side.

2. Use the Maryland flag on the previous page, or create your own design. Draw the flag pattern with bold lines to show through the layered freezer paper and fabric. Trace the lines with a pencil onto the right side of the fabric using a lightbox.

3. Go over the pencil lines with a black Pigma .01 pen. Use a light touch so the ink doesn't bleed. Heat set the ink by ironing, leaving the freezer paper on the back.

4. Start with a light color. For our example, dip a size 0 round (very fine) brush in yellow soft body acrylic paint and wipe the excess paint off the brush on the rim of the bottle. Paint the center of an outlined area. Then carefully paint from the black edge to the yellow. Heat set after each color.

5. Rinse the brush clean. Repeat Step 4 for the remaining colors.

6. After all the colors have been painted and heat set, cut out the shape, adding a seam allowance as you cut. Baste the motif in place on the background fabric, then appliqué.

Acrylic Inks

How does the acrylic ink differ from the acrylic paint? Soft body acrylic paint holds its line cleanly on dry fabric, leaving brilliant color with just one coat.

Acrylic ink is more liquid and works more like dye. After a motif has been outlined in pen, start painting ink in the center of a motif, to confine the bleed, then use a dip pen to draw a clean line touching the black pen outline. Layer ink coats to achieve the desired density and vibrancy.

Butterfly by Tina Cole. Painted using acrylic inks. *Photo by Matthew Cole*

EXERCISE: LAYER AND BLEND COLORS WITH ACRYLIC PAINTS AND INKS

1. Using the butterfly photo above as a guide, draw the butterfly (or other motif) with a thicker line using a black Pigma .08 pen. Heat set the ink by ironing. Apply paint or ink (Raw Sienna in this case) to the center wing section. Moisten the butterfly wing with a cotton swab. This allows the yellow–brown color to bleed outward for translucence. Use a tiny dip pen to fill in the raggedy bleed adjacent to the outlines. Remember to heat set after each color is applied.

2. Select another color and lighten it with white, applying it in the section next to the first color. Use a size 0 round brush and acrylic paint to add nonoutlined second layers. Heat set, then go over the inked lines as needed and heat set again. The motif will be cut out so any bleeding into the margin will be turned under with the seam allowance.

3. Embellish the painted butterfly with a fillip of embroidery. Or go further: Outline stitch the black lines with one strand of embroidery floss. Add iridescent touches using DMC Light Effects floss with its glisten of flickering highlights. To Baltimoreans, butterflies symbolized "life of the soul"—an evocative image in any cra.

Baltimore's Oriole in an Apple Tree by Tina Cole. Bird, apples, and butterfly painted by Approach 1. This original pattern is based on the tree in the traditional Peacock Pastorale (Pattern 14, page 99). What a joy to be able to paint any bird into your needleart with Tina's inspiration and Approach 1! *Photo by Matthew Cole*

APPROACH 2: STARTING WITH WET FABRIC

With this method, you paint wet yardage, then cut it and manipulate it (ruching, folding). Or use it with an appliqué window template (page 65) to capture the ideal section of painted appliqué fabric for the appliqué motif.

Principles of Approach 2

- Wet cloth encourages bleeding, the seeping out of color, that gives Baltmores a painterly, shaded look.

- Ink, being thinner, bleeds more easily than paint, but both work. The closer you place two colors (for example, a drop of red placed ¾″ away from a drop of yellow), the more intense will be the blend color between them. And vice versa, the further apart, the less intense.

- Paint or ink can be applied by daubing with a crumpled paper towel, a fragment of sponge, or a brush stroke. It can also be lifted off by these means. And it can be spattered or painted in drops. You'll think of more!

- A *window template* is the paper frame (the window) from which an appliqué shape's pattern (template) is cut. Cut out your pattern from freezer paper, creating an "open window" on the paper. Use the open window to find the area of cloth you wish to use for the appliqué.

EXERCISE: PAINT FABRIC FOR ROSEBUDS AND RUCHING

Lyre Wreath in Bloom (Pattern 8, page 93). An invitation to play: painting circles into rosebuds and bias strips into ruching!

Preparation

1. Prewash (preshrink) a fat quarter of muslin by bringing it to boil in a microwave. Iron the fabric dry.

2. Make a template from Pattern B in Lyre Wreath in Bloom (page 93) using either a Sakura Gelly Roll gold metallic pen or a Pigma .01 pen. Iron to heat set. Note: Draw the pattern at the top of the cloth, leaving the rest to paint and cut in ¾″ bias strips for shell ruching (page 79).

3. Drench the cloth in water, then roll it between terry towels until it is not dripping but is still very wet.

4. Look at the photo at right. Consider how those rosebud circles (shown folded in half on the bias) must have been painted. To make a yellow rosebud center, paint yellow at the center of the circle using paint or ink. To make the right half

of the rose dark, paint the right side of the circle with color mixed in a separate container (red, yellow, perhaps some white). Then paint the other side with a lighter color version (paint or ink cut with more white or water). Cut out a circle with 1″ extra all around. Finger-press the rosebud folds (page 77). Open, then paint along the folds.

Experiment! Easiest of all is to paint the remainder of the fat quarter for ruching strips, experimenting to your heart's content. At the back of your mind, think how you might paint in serpentine stripes to apply another time to fruit and roses cut with a window template.

Lyre Wreath in Bloom (Pattern 8, page 93) by Tina Cole. Tina painted the rose's ruched center and the folded buds using Approach 2. *Photo by Matthew Cole*

EXERCISE: CREATE PAINTED FABRIC EFFECTS

You can create or imitate almost any fabric effect you wish. Experiment using both Approach 1—Dry Cloth (page 43), with the option of wetting a specific bleed area with a cotton swab, and Approach 2 (page 45). Below are a handful of effects to try with baskets or vases of fruits and flowers.

After painting a piece of fabric, use a window template (page 65) to locate the most realistic shading for any given flower or fruit. Paint curves to achieve a rounded shadow. Painting an undulating line with a small sponge brush gives mirrored curves. A cleft fruit (peach, plum) needs dark side/light side window templates (see page 47).

Epergne of Fruit (similar to Pattern 24, page 109) by Tina Cole.

Urn of Flowers by Tina Cole.

Fruit with a curved fruit shadow from Epergne of Fruit; see Painting a Cleft Fruit (page 47).

Rose from Tina Cole's Clipper Ship, using a window template (page 65) allows for finding the perfect shading for each petal.

Coneflowers: Use a dry brush to sparingly apply soft body acrylic paint in separately mixed shades of yellow to orange. Heat set the lighter colors before the darker mix is applied. This can give a stripy effect to flower petals like cosmos or coneflower, rather than a smooth blending of shades.

Center Medallion from *Happy Hours, Sweetly Spent*, Goose girl teaches a young friend to sew in Jackson Hole, WY by Marla Duenwald Landt (quilt on page 20). Marla has cleverly depicted the beautiful background of the Tetons and valley using Pigma pen outline and a painted wash using Approach 2: Starting with Wet Fabric (page 45).

Plump rounded petals: Paint a magenta horseshoe shape, and wet the center with a cotton swab (without heat setting). With a brush of the magenta paint cut way back with white, pull the edge of magenta out to the opening.

Epergne and Urn photos by Matthew Cole

PAINTING A CLEFT FRUIT

This technique is very similar to Stencil Shading using oil pastels (page 48). Our example is from Basket of Fruit and Flowers (Pattern 23, page 108).

1. Stabilize a square of fabric by ironing freezer paper to the wrong side.

2. Trace a cleft fruit, including the cleft line, onto the dull side of a square of freezer paper. Make a registration mark on each half of the fruit. Cut out the fruit and cut it apart on the cleft line so you have the window template where the fruit was cut out, the left half of the fruit, and the right half of the fruit.

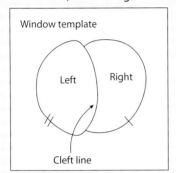

3. Place the window template and the right side of the cut-out freezer paper on the right side of the fabric. Use an iron to press the freezer paper into place.

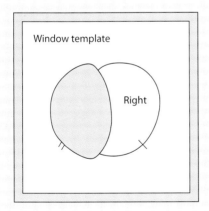

4. Use paint right out of the jar and a dry brush to apply the lightest shade first. Don't use water or the paint will seep under the freezer paper.

5. Then apply the medium shade, and then the darkest, blending the colors on the fabric.

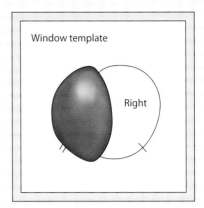

6. After the paint has dried (if needed, use a hair dryer to speed drying), remove the right side freezer paper. Place the left side freezer paper in place and iron it down. As before, paint the lightest, then medium, then darkest colors using paint right out of the jar.

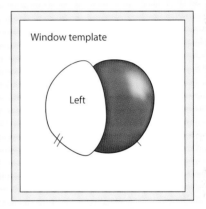

7. Let the paint dry and remove the freezer paper from the front and back of the fabric. Follow the paint manufacturer's recommendation and, if needed, heat set the color to ensure colorfastness. Cut out the appliqué shape, adding a ⅛″ seam allowance all around. Appliqué the fruit to the background, adding a stem-well circle—a classic Baltimore design concept.

8. Add a line of topstitching along the cleft seam to add depth after it is appliquéd in place.

Clipper Ship (Pattern 25, page 110) by Tina Cole. The Maryland flag was painted using Approach 1 (page 43) and the flowers in the garland were painted using Approach 2 (page 45), the perfect petals being found by window templates. The American flag (here appliquéd) is not only the most common flag rendition of the Baltimore era, but would be so easy for you to paint on cotton by Approach 1, then add colonial knot thread stars.
Photo by Matthew Cole

The Princess of the Orient stencil-shaded appliqué by Linda Cox.
Photo by Linda Cox

Stencil-shaded appliquéd clipper ship by Evelyn Crovo Hall.
Photo by Evelyn Crovo Hall

Stencil Shading

Stencil Shading with oil pastels gives appliqué dimension and a mysterious beauty. Stencil Shading is not for items that will be heavily laundered—it may fade slightly in washing but does not bleed. The pigment is in the oil and is intransient—we have centuries-old oil paintings. The highest-oil-content pastels in my experience, Sakura's Specialist, go on more smoothly and fade dramatically less in washing than either Sakura's next grade down or other good pastel brands I've used. For wall quilts and heirloom Albums, the effect of stencil shading echoes Old Baltimore's look delightfully!

EXERCISE: LEARN THE BASIC STENCIL SHADING OIL PASTEL TECHNIQUE

1. Use a layered rose from the Baltimore Clipper Ship and garland (Pattern 25, page 110). Stabilize the wrong side of a 6″ × 6″ square of the lighter shade of the rose appliqué fabric by ironing freezer paper to the wrong side.

2. Make a perforated window template (page 65) of your rose onto the dull side of a 3½″ × 3½″ square of freezer paper.

Cut out the individual rose petals, leaving the rose's printed outline on the rose petal template. (This widens the window template a pencil line's worth, all around.)

3. Iron the perforated window template (your *stencil*), centered, shiny side down on the right side of the rose fabric.

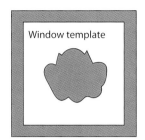

4. The window template is now your artist's palette. Scribble dime-sized dots of dark red and purple oil pastel onto the window template frame. Replace petals 2–6, taping them lightly in place with repositionable tape.

5. Pull a 5″ × 5″ scrap of muslin over your forefinger. Beginning with the lighter color, push the oil pastel over the edge of the template, onto the appliqué fabric for petal 1, working the color inward approximately ⅓″ or so. Push hardest just inside the edge of the template, and then taper off the pressure until you've achieved the desired shading. Continue in this fashion, scribbling more color on the template as needed, and working from the lighter color (red) to the darker color (purple). The lighter color serves as a blender. Push the purple harder when you cross the edge, and lighten up slightly as you move away from the edge. This gives the stenciled look.

Stencil shading a rose petal

6. Replace petal 1 and remove petal 2. Similarly, stencil shade petal 2 and then repeat for petals 3–6. When the rose is all stenciled, cut it out with a ³⁄₁₆″ seam allowance all around. Remove the templates and backing and heat set with a tissue press cloth. Appliqué the outside edge of the rose. Optimally, topstitch quilt or embroider the petal outlines. Repeat Steps 2–5 for the outer petals.

Detail of Clipper Ship Garland Rose (complete block on page 48). Although cut with a window template from a commercial print, this is exactly the dimensional look achieved by window stencil shading with dark purple oil pastel on vibrant red. Notice the lazy daisy stitched leaf edging and the pistil and the stitched and clustered colonial knots center. Particularly beatiful is Evelyn's stem-stitched fern center vein, edged with lazy daisy louops, punctuated with glass seed beads, and topped with grape-like bunches of single-strand colonial knots. *Photo by Evelyn Crovo Hall*

EXERCISE: EMBELLISH FRUIT WITH PASTEL STENCIL SHADING

If the fruit is uncleft, like an apple, follow Steps 1–5 and remove the window template.

If the fruit is cleft, such as a peach or plum, cut the template apart along the cleft line. Put the right side back into the window after Step 3, above. Stencil shade the edges of the left side.

Next, remove the left-hand template while you replace the right. Stencil shade the left side. Remove the window templates and heat set the color. (See page 45 for using this technique with paint.)

Photo Silhouette Portraits

Eight silhouette portraits shine through porthole-like blocks (Pattern 11, page 96) in *Happiness Is in the Journey*. Effective quilt design and precious family history! A silhouette (a filled outline) makes perfect quilt art portraits when stencil-shaded by the window template method.

If you'd like to watch Elly herself at work making a silhouette of her grandson Elias, see her DVD Elly Sienkiewicz Teaches You Beginning Appliqué *(see Sources, page 126).*

SINGLE SHAPE SILHOUETTE

1. To center a silhouette in the Family History Block (Pattern 11, page 96), take a side view photo of your subject: Have the person stand with her or his right shoulder to the wall, looking up at the far corner of the ceiling for perfect posture! Move in toward the subject until the head fills the camera window.

2. To create the silhouette template, photocopy the portrait photo (or print it digitally), and turning the picture facedown on a piece of fabric on a lightbox, trace the silhouette artistically on the paper's unprinted side with a fine-point mechanical pencil.

3. Make a window template as described on page 65. Draw the head into a graceful outline to be filled.

4. Using a Pigma .01 pen, outline, then stencil shade to fill first the hair and collar, then more lightly the face and neck.

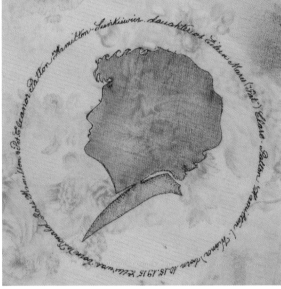

Self-portrait in pen and pastel stencil shading, by Elly Sienkiewicz. Note how the fabric print has been used to suggest curls, and words in Copperplate calligraphy (page 51) are used to frame the silhouette. We've now learned that once again, eyelashes, which would not have been on the photo, are difficult. Can you see a shadow of an eye properly placed by the cloth's print on Elly's cheek here—as in Little Ellie's portrait? (at right)
Photo by Elly Sienkiewicz

MULTISHAPE SILHOUETTE

Masses of loose, long hair can make a silhouette difficult to read. A solution is to cut the silhouette template (see Single Shape Silhouette Steps 1 and 2, above) into multiple (hair/body) shapes.

1. Stabilize the background square by adhering freezer paper to the wrong side of the fabric. Adhere the window template (portrait removed) to the right side of the fabric. Now outline each window on the background with a black Pigma .01 pen.

2. Cut the 1-piece portrait template into 4 pieces: 2 head/shoulder templates and 2 hair templates. Adhere the head/shoulder templates one at a time to the right side of the fabric. Pen the outline between the flesh and hair. Stencil shade the 2 hair areas (page 48).

3. Remove the head/shoulder templates. Adhere the 2 hair templates and stencil shade the head/shoulders. Pen shade (page 53) the edges as desired with dots and etching lines.

Family History Block (Pattern 11, page 96) Portrait of Little Ellie at Eight, by Elly Sienkiewicz. The hair was stenciled in two separate windows framing the face.

NOTE

Sharing hindsight may benefit your portraits: While the silhouette of Little Ellie was traced from the reverse of a photo, it made her look older. This is entirely the fault of the penned eyelash—not the photo. Today, I would not pen in Little Ellie's eyelashes. The snapshot did not show eyelashes, but where I added them made this 8-year-old look much older, in fact, just like her then 30-year-old aunt! Coincidentally, a dark spot in the print appears where an 8-year-old's eye really should be—lower and to the left. Can you see the child in this portrait?

Silhouettes can also be done beautifully in Ultrasuede (page 60), using a single layer of Ultrasuede or multiple layers. Below is a portrait of Katya as young girl, done in two layers—face/shoulders (with a ⅛″ underlap) and a top layer of hair.

Portrait of Katya by Elly Sienkiewicz, done with layered Ultrasuede. *Fancy Appliqué* (C&T Publishing). *Photo by Sharon Risdorph*

Another approach to portraits was taken by Evelyn van der Heiden. The silhouettes were done by photo / template / oil pastel shading (rather than the window template). Evelyn typed the inscription in Adobe Bickham Script, similar to Copperplate but the capitals are more ornamental. Using black and brown Pigma pens in sizes .005, .01, and .05, she outlined the empty silhouette space with lines and dots (page 53). To stabilize the fabric for inking, she sprayed and ironed Magic Sizing on the underside of the block. Using a lightbox, the printed words guided her hand-inking.

Portrait of Our Sons, by Evelyn van der Heiden. Hand-traced calligraphy from a printout of Adobe Bickham Script, similar to Copperplate, but the capitals are more ornamental. Notice how Evelyn (like Elly on page 50) uses penned dots to outline the silhouettes. *Photo by Evelyn van der Heiden*

Copperplate Calligraphy

This eighteenth- and nineteenth-century script based on English Round Hand is the direct ancestor of Palmer Script. So many of us born mid-twentieth century, were taught to write in Palmer Script: A slanted hand with its upper-case twice the height of its lowercase. Notice two essential differences between Palmer Hand (not pictured) and the Copperplate Alphabet (pictured):

Copperplate Round Hand Alphabet by Horace G. Healey, used with permission of Zaner-Bloser, Inc.

The Copperplate uppercase is three times the height of the lowercase, and every downstroke is thickened. This comes from the Copperplate's elbow pen, so flexible that when pulled for a downstroke the tines open, letting out more ink. You can buy an elbow pen and Higgins' eternal black India Ink at an art store. The comparison with the black Pigma .01 pen (nonbleeding in my experience) used in this chapter's illustrations will fill you with gratitude! Pigmas are permanent and intransient; they are *archival* (acid-free is a paper term), that is, they have no ill effect long-term and are used by the Library of Congress for marking documents and prints.

 Thickening the Downstroke

Thickening the downstroke (or where the pen drags, as in the tail flourish) imitates in Pigma pen the look of Copperplate calligraphy. As might be used in a grape tendril, don't you agree, this thickening makes the line more expressive, artistic, and antique looking?

Roses for Hans Christian Andersen (Pattern 1, page 86) with Copperplate calligraphed frame, by Elly Sienkiewicz. *Photo by Sharon Risedorph*

Another example of beautiful writing from *Faith, Hope, and Love* by Suzanne Louth and Denise Clausen (full quilt on page 22)

NOTE

The Roses for Hans Christian Andersen block, with its Copperplate calligraphed frame, is based on a symmetrical papercut pattern that is overlaid by dimensional buds, belying how easy it is to make by Cutaway Appliqué! (See page 32 for Cutaway Appliqué step by easy step.) It is the first pattern in our book, meaning it has been chosen as the best place to start. Moreover it has a free downloadable lesson plan on www.ctpub.com inviting all to teach it to students who have this book.

Roses for Hans Christian Andersen teaches basic appliqué in a most appealing, systematic way and includes layered and dimensional appliqué. There are delightful models in *Happiness Is in the Journey*. If you prefer a rather sophisticated interpretation, consider a calligraphed frame.

EXERCISE: EMBELLISH A BLOCK BY ENCIRCLING THE CENTER WITH A COPPERPLATE INSCRIPTION.

1. Make a master layout: Place a copy of the pattern on a lightbox. Use a compass to pencil-draw the circle that will become the writing line. Photocopy-enlarge the Copperplate alphabet (page 51) to the appropriate size. With a fine mechanical pencil, lightly pencil-trace the inscription, letter by letter, off the enlarged alphabet and onto the master. Finalize the writing with a black .05 Pigma pen so it is quite visible over the lightbox, under the cloth.

2. Prepare the appliquéd block fabric for tracing the words, as follows: Spray Magic Sizing to the wrong side of the fabric to stiffen it. Press using a tissue pressing cloth. This sizing, mostly polyester, inhibits ink bleed and does not attract bugs. Fold the block lightly in quarters, pin-matching the center and fold lines to those of the circle master, which you place behind the appliquéd block. To prevent shifting, pin the paper to the cloth.

3. To inscribe, trace each letter onto the fabric. When all are traced, go back and thicken the downstrokes. Heat set, using a tissue pressing cloth.

Calligraphy means "beautiful writing." It is a such an elegant embellishment for our heirloom appliqué and surprisingly simple to learn on your own.

Drama with Dynamic Dots!

Penned dots are a favorite way to transit gently from the solidity of the appliqué to the openness of the background. I like to cluster dots densely as they outline a silhouette, or even to ornament the outline bordering the empty space of a silhouette and then thin out in venturing beyond that border.

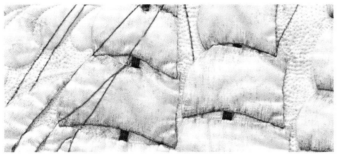

Mary Tozer used penned dots and lines on the sails of her clipper ship (Pattern 25, page 110) to give dimension. Sails are outlined in 1 strand of YLI taupe silk 6-strand floss using a stem stitch. Complete block is in *Happiness Is in the Journey* (page 12).

Not only do dots come inked, but they can also be embroidered knots.

Peacock Pastorale (Pattern 14, page 99), by Elly Sienkiewicz. This fancywork interpretation of the Peacock Pastorale block uses colonial knots (page 57) done in 4mm silk ribbon embroidery (in yellow, at left) instead of inked dots to add detail in open spaces. The colonial knots add visual texture along with the other stitchery: leaf-stitched silk ribbon leaves and tree trunk (its variegated color range imitates Baltimore's painterly look).

Photo by Teri Young

Heat-Transferred Engraving

You can transfer copies of line art made on many home photocopiers and faxes (not printers). The banderole (page 54) appears on an antebellum Baltimore. Found on a calling card at an antique mall, this graphic can now embellish your own quilt! So can computer-designed letter graphics and even drawn silhouettes of buildings or people.

The Maryland Statehouse in a Rose of Sharon Wreath, by Elly Sienkiewicz. The statehouse was a photocopy ironed onto the background cloth.
Photo by Teri Young. Block from Elly's portfolio (no pattern available).

You can transfer copies of line drawings on many home photocopiers and faxes (not injet printers). The most basic commercial photocopiers also transfer. Technology is changing so try a sample if you aren't sure about the copier. Instructions for using a simple home or office copier follow:

1. Cut a roughly 4″ × 4″ square of freezer paper and iron it, centered and shiny side down, to the wrong side of the background square.

2. Photocopy the banderole (page 54), and trim it to a ½″ white margin all around.

3. Hold the photocopy to the light and fold it (printed side in) in quarters, creasing it to show the vertical and horizontal centers.

4. Pin the photocopy to the background [a] (2 pins [b] at the top, to let in the iron), copied side down and with creases [c] aligned with the background's quadrant creases [d].

5. Use a dry, hot iron (set to Linen), and iron on a hard surface. Lift the back end of the iron so that the pressure is hardest on the front end of the iron. Press with a heavy motion to encourage the carbon on the paper to transfer to the fabric. If the iron is scorching hot, protect the background with a tissue abutting the photocopy. If the iron is not hot enough, the photocopy will not transfer.

6. Without removing the pins, lift a corner of the photocopy to see if the print has transferred. If the transfer is not clear, iron hotter and harder. You need enough of an image to be able to draw over it and clarify it.

7. Leave the freezer paper ironed to the back of the background while you go over the photocopy-transferred banderole with a black Pigma .01 pen. Make small, engraving-like pen strokes, covering all the impermanent photocopy lines with freshly inked lines.

8. After inscribing the banderole's center, heat set the ink, using a tissue as a pressing cloth. Once you complete the pressing, remove the stabilizing freezer paper from underneath the fabric.

While Elly's inkwork in the original Roses for Hans Christian Andersen block (Pattern 1, page 86) is complex, this banderole (at left) traced and ironed on, is easy enough for a first-time album block.

Detail of Star Ruched Rose (Pattern 12, page 96) by Janice Vaine. Heat-transferred engraving and calligraphy (page 53).

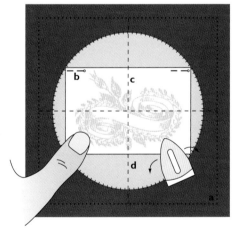

Place photocopied image wrong side up, and press to transfer image.

Banderole

Embroidery Stitches

This is a small posy of embroidery stitches and embellishments pictured on Album Quilt blocks.

TOPSTITCH

Baltimore Urn of Fruit and Blessings by Elly Sienkiewicz.
The blue plum is topstitched down the center, as is the green leaf on the left. However, the apparent topstitching on the pineapple has been penned in. The stem circle is from Ultrasuede, and the leaves are fussy cut and ink embellished. Embroidered apple stem is blanket stitch over red fabric appliqué. *Photo by Teri Young*

Top-stitching is a running stitch that looks like a quilting stitch done in sewing thread or a strand of embroidery floss. It is taken through the appliqué and into and out of the background cloth. This stitch can draw the veins on ovate leaves or the fingers on a hand. You could also top-stitch a rose to define its petals in more detail. Above, top-stitch helps define the cleft in a stenciled blue plum.

Detail from Baltimore Urn of Fruit and Blessings shows topstitched leaves and Kathy Dunigan's skinny-skinny stems (page 63), inked rose moss, and ultrasuede over ribbon appliqué (page 61)

COUCHING

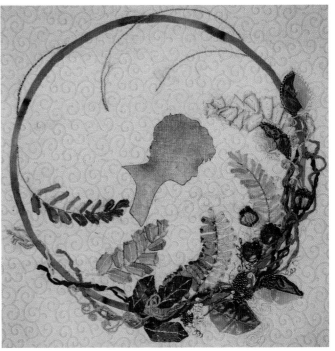

A block in progress, Elly's self-portrait as a young woman includes bias silk stem overlaid with couched threads, ferns made with stem-stitched center spine leafed out in silk ribbon, and leaf-stitched embroidery.
Photo by Teri Young

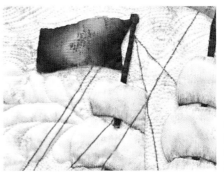

Couched rigging from Baltimore Clipper Ship and Garland (Pattern 25, page 110) by Mary Tozer.

This is an amazingly useful embroidery technique. With a single strand of floss, you can draw a fine line. With a double strand or a strand of #8 perle cotton, you can draw a thicker line (even rig a clipper ship!). You can stitch on fine trims with this. Use thread to stitch down the floss or perle cotton.

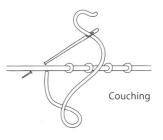

Couching

Baltimore's Iconic Eagle (Pattern 15, page 100) by Sandy Butler

OUTLINE STITCH

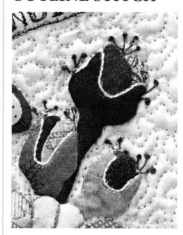

Outline stitch

Detail from Baltimore's Iconic Eagle

The following mnemonic device might help you remember the difference between these two sister stitches:

Stem **S**titch = thread **S**wung low

Outline stitch = thread **O**verhead

STEM STITCH

Detail from Baltimore's Iconic Eagle

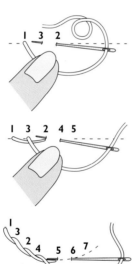

Stem stitch

Turning stem stitch corner

FRENCH KNOT

This is a simple knot, especially when compared with the colonial knot (page 57). It can be one wrap or multiple wraps.

Detail from Peacock Pastorale by Elly Sienkiewicz (full block on page 53)

Calyx centers of French knots from ⅛" woven silk ribbon.
Photo by Teri Young

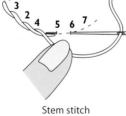

French knot

Legged French Knot and the Pistil Stitch

Detail from Baltimore's Iconic Eagle

To give added texture and dimension to the rosebuds, try adding botanical details at the top edges. To do this, use a single strand of floss and make a straight stitch (page 60), ending at the wrong side of the fabric. Come back up to the right side, one or two threads away from the end of the straight stitch. Make a French knot with 2 wraps of the thread. Group these with stylized details as you wish.

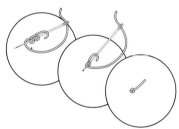

Legged French knot botanical details

A variation of this technique, called the pistil stitch, involves stitching a short line of stem stitches (page 56), ending on the back. Come up a few threads away and make a colonial knot (this page) at the end of the stem stitches. Evelyn Crovo Hall used this stitch combination at the flower center of her rose garland.

Detail from clipper ship block by Evelyn Crovo Hall (full block on page 71). Colonial knots are foam, lifted on stem stitch rills, rising from the Good Ship's wake. Yellow colonial knot dots dance among stem stitch stems sprouting gold beads and lazy daisy stitch and at their tip, single strand French knot cluster flowers, vibrant in purple. The great surprise are the pink blanket stitched circles, like cross-slices of orange, but pink!

COLONIAL KNOT

Detail from clipper ship block by Robyn MacKay. Fuchsia colonial knots stitched with size 3 pearl cotton cascade, forming vivid flowers. Robyn's fern (stem stitch with lazy daisy stitch in 2 strands of 6 strand cotton floss), Pigma brown pen-inked leaf veins, and Showy Ruched Ribbon Roses (page 81) make this a garland to talk about!

The colonial knot tends to be a more uniform shape (like a donut on a plate) than a French knot. Make a figure eight over the needle, as shown, for the most well-behaved knot. Add another wrap or two for a larger knot. Robyn MacKay's cascades of heavy variegated floss colonial knots, pictured above, look like a favorite Baltimore era flower that most closely resembles Love-lies-bleeding.

Colonial knot, one wrap   Colonial knot, two wraps

The MacKay Clan, Clipper Ship (Pattern 25, page 110) by Robyn MacKay. What a glory! Her flags a-flying, she sails above a lush garland of Showy Ruched Ribbon Roses (page 81); stem stitch and lazy daisy greenery; and dramtaic fuchsia-colored colonial knots forming that old-fashioned flower, Love Lies Bleeding. *Photo by Robyn MacKay*

CHAIN STITCH

Detail from A Hero's Crown (Dove and Anchor) block (Pattern 20, page 105) by Diane DeVido Tetreault. Cleverly, Diane stitched this anchor chain in size 3 perle cotton.

This stitch is easier to control than the stem or outline stitch.

Chain stitch

SATIN STITCH

Detail from A Hero's Crown by Bette Augustine.

Begin with an outline on fabric. Using a milliner's #10 needle with a single strand of 6-strand floss, stitch up one line, down on the other. Make close, parallel stitches. Optional: Outline stitch (page 56) first. Pad the shape with parallel stitches perpendicular to the top layer's covering stitches.

Satin stitch

CAUGHT THREAD STITCH

Use a new milliner's/straw #10 needle and machine-weight thread (DMC cotton works well) in a high-contrast color. Begin with a knot on the back and bring the thread to the right side. Take a small stitch and slip the tip of the needle under 2 to 3 threads of the background fabric. Catch these threads on the needle and push the needle forward another stitch length. Again, catch 2 to 3 threads: slip the needle under them and up to the surface again. This caught thread in effect couches the needle-drawn thread. Try this for a tracery of rose moss or tendrils as well as delicate inscriptions or signatures. Experiment with threads including single strands of silk floss.

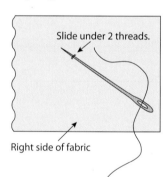

Slide under 2 threads.

Right side of fabric

Caught-thread stitch

A Hero's Crown (Dove and Anchor) by Betty Augustine (Pattern 20, page 105). Here's a bevy of embellishment details! From the colonial knots (page 57) in the dove's beak made with 50-weight variegated DMC machine appliqué thread to a plethora of these same knots forming the buds. Then in a brilliant personal touch, Bette entwines the wreath with a miniature vine stem stitched (page 56) with a single strand of taupe DMC rayon floss … and more berries.

BLANKET STITCH

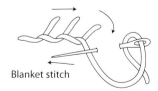

Kick-out blanket stitch

The traditional blanket stitch is a revived 1930s appliqué classic, recently popular because of the ease of fused appliqué. Done by hand or machine, the blanket stitch protects the raw edges of the fused appliqué (page 60), just as it protects a buttonhole or the raw edge of a blanket. This so-easy stitch is an embellishment favorite of mine: I've dubbed "kick-out blanket stitch" a realistic detail to evoke the serrated edge of a rose leaf. Its length lies ⅛″ inside the leaf edge. Its leg kicks out beyond the edge, onto the background. Importantly, this leg always slants toward the point of the leaf or the moss or fern: For if one stitches the kick-out blanket stitch up the left side and down the right, it becomes stitched ferns or rose moss.

Blanket stitch

Double blanket stitch

EMBROIDERED ROSE MOSS

The Gift of a Rose, by Elly Sienkiewicz, from *Romancing Ribbon with Flowers*. Notice the rose moss in cotton and in gold metallic? This is a glorious example of fused appliqué with blanket stitch. *Photo by Teri Young*

The newly hybridized rose moss came from England to America in the 1840s, where it became a stitched favorite. Depending on scale or style, the "moss" of this sweet-smelling rose was inked or embroidered. It added a realistic touch, and witnessed the good ladies' enthusiasm for what the Victorians called "reading the pencil of God." Ink the lush moss with a black Pigma .01 pen, or embroider it by blanket stitching in one strand of 50- or 60-weight sewing thread. Pencil the moss stems first, or simply stitch them freehand. Righthanders start on the left at the rose, blanket stitch the desired length, then turn the block around and continue the blanket stitch down the other side. The key is that the legs of the stitch must all slant toward the stem. If they were perpendicular to the center stem, you'd have a centipede.

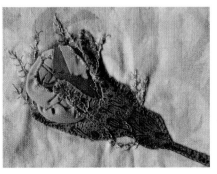

FUSIBLE APPLIQUÉ

What is Fusible Appliqué? Suitable for almost any of the Baltimore blocks, this simplest of all appliqué techniques uses paper-backed fusible web. The pattern is traced on the paper side, fused to the wrong side of the appliqué fabric, cut out on the drawn line (no seam allowance added), and fused to the background fabric (once the paper is removed). Follow the manufacturer's simple directions to use Wonder Under, Heat*n*Bond Lite, or a similar product.

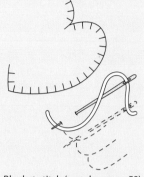

Blanket stitch (see also page 59)

STRAIGHT STITCH

The straight stitch embellishment dances through antique Baltimores. Needleturn baste first, then straight stitch (milliner's 10 needle, 1 strand floss for smaller blocks, 2 strands for larger blocks) as illustrated.

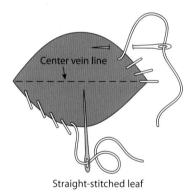

Center vein line

Straight-stitched leaf

Faithful replica of a straight-stitched Album block from Baltimore's German immigrant Numsen family.
Photo by Teri Young

Needleturn Basting

Sometimes the seam of a needleturned leaf must be turned and held under before you edge-embroider it with a stitch (blanket, lazy daisy, or straight stitch). This, even though that stitch itself attaches (appliqués) the leaf to background. Needleturn basting uses the rolling under and tack stitch of needleturn appliqué (page 32) but instead of 10 stitches per inch, take just 3 or 4—fewer on a straight or gentle curve, more on a tight curve. Use a milliner's/straw #11 needle and 100-weight silk thread so that the almost invisible tack-stitch basting doesn't need removing.

Ultrasuede Appliqué

Ultrasuede is washable synthetic suede. It needs no added seam allowance, so it is spectacularly easy for sewing appliqués. Because it is polyurethane, however, it must be ironed gingerly (lightly and quickly) with a dry iron set to Synthetic. Ultrasuede has a right side (the brighter, nappier side), and you sew it with the same thread and the same tack stitch as for cotton appliqué. I use #10 Richard Hemmings milliner's or chisel-pointed Ultrasuede Needles (see Sources, page 126) to hand stitch. The following explains how to sew single-layer Ultrasuede apples to the Family Tree House block (Pattern 5, page 90) or the squirrel in Squirrel's Berry Breakfast (Pattern 6, page 91).

1. Use self-stick label paper to make a template. Alternatively, iron at low temperature and very lightly a freezer paper template, shiny side down, to the right side of the Ultrasuede.

2. Add no seam allowance as you cut out the apple/circle, guided by the paper. Remove the paper.

3. Dab gluestick on the fabric background within the drawn apple shape. Press down on the apple to adhere it to the background.

4. Sew the appliqué in place with a fine tack stitch.

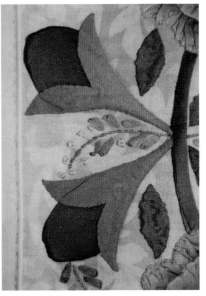

Detail from the Maryland Statehouse in a Rose of Sharon Wreath by Elly Sienkiewicz (full block on page 53). Ultrasuede on Ribbon Appliqué, stem stitched stem, and bias-cut silk ribbon (with raw edge showing) for wreath stem.
Photo by Teri Young

Family Tree House block (Pattern 5, page 90). Connie Mooers enlarged her Ultrasuede apples with two rows (sometimes different shades) of fine two-strand floss chain stitches (page 58), thereby adding an embellishment to be enjoyed by hearts yet unborn.

ULTRASUEDE ON ULTRASUEDE

On an acorn, for example, cut the cap with no seam allowance added. Add ⅛″ underlap, though, to the top of the nut where it lies beneath the cap. Stitch both layers as described for Ultrasuede Appliqué (page 60).

ULTRASUEDE ON RIBBON APPLIQUÉ

1. Draw the shape (a bud for example) on a 1″–1½″ French shaded wired ribbon (wires removed).

2. Paint clear nail polish along the outside line of the added seam allowance. Allow the polish to dry.

3. Cut out the bud shape with the seam allowance. Silk pin or baste the bud in place on the background. Or gluestick baste (page 28)—but only under the seam allowance.

4. Appliqué the portion of the bud that will be outside the calyx.

5. Cut the calyx with no seams added out of Ultrasuede (page 60). Dab glue in the drawn outline of the calyx on the background; press it into place. Appliqué all of the exposed edges. In the example, a piece of thin batting, cut ⅛″ smaller all around than the bud shape, was adhered to the background with gluestick to pad the bud before the ribbon cover was appliquéd down.

Another version of Basket of Flowers (Pattern 13, page 98) by Elly Sienkiewicz. Acorns done by Ultrasuede on Ultrasuede, leaves in cotton, velvet ribbon, pierced leaf stitched in 4mm silk ribbon embroidered stem and leaf.

Stems for Flora, Stems for Weaving

Like our fascination with "perfect grapes" (page 67), we're on the perfect stem search. For example, Superfine Stems (below) are perfect for wreaths, but not for weaving. There are two families of stems: Stems Made on a Foundation (below) and Stems Made in-Hand (at right). Stems Made on a Foundation can be used for almost anything except weaving. Stems Made in-Hand can be used for anything. Great! But what are the drawbacks? The stems Made in-Hand take more appliqué stitches, and for certain tasks they are not the simplest way. For all stems, make your life easy by cutting on the bias for curves and on the straight (more economical) for noncurves.

For example, I'd make a flagpole by the Superfine Stems method; you might do it differently. Let's meet cousins in each family—you'll come to know when to use each and which cousin works best for you!

STEMS MADE ON A FOUNDATION

Superfine Stems

Stems, which I have dubbed Superfine Stems, can be made in-hand (page 62) or on the background, such as this one for a wreath. The fact that this stem started with such an easy-to-handle strip (1″ wide) charmed me, while the secret to making it superfine is Step 5.

1. Cut a 1″ × 24″ bias strip of cotton and fold it in half lengthwise, right sides out.

2. Gently place the bias strip on the background cloth—do not pull it. Orient the fold toward the wreath center with the raw edges right on top of the drawn stem line. Pin the folded strip every 1″, beginning and ending under a yet-to-come flower. When finished, the folded side will stretch to cover the larger outside of the circle.

3. Use fine running stitches to stitch a scant ³⁄₁₆″ away from and parallel to the raw edges.

4. This is a test: Place a straight pin where you plan to stitch the first running stitch. Finger-press the fold hard up against the pin and over the raw edges. If the folded edge doesn't cover the line and raw edges, adjust the pin so that the line and raw edges are covered. If the fold covers the raw edges

and drawn line, stitch a running stitch around the circle, then begin tack stitching it down, and continue full circle.

5. *The secret formula: The width of the finished stem equals the distance from the running stitches to the fold.* To cover the raw edge, make sure the distance to the fold is a bit wider than the distance from the stitches to the raw edges. If the running stitches follow a line ⅛″ parallel to the fold, you can finish (after trimming off the excess) with a ⅛″-wide stem.

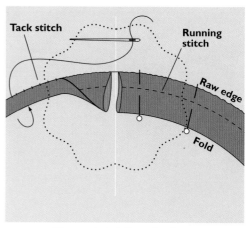

Place and stitch Superfine Stem.

Superfine Stems are excellent, but they have to be sewn to the background as you make them. They can't be woven into baskets or arranged freely to fill a vase. To do this, you need premade stems (Stems Made in-Hand, below).

STEMS MADE IN-HAND

Trifold Stem

Marjorie Mahoney taught me this wonderfully easy stem—by phone! You could use this trifold, basted strip to make any stem. In addition—and this is big—you can also use it to weave a basket or to sew a meandering stem of inside and outside curves (as on a border). Simply sew the inside curves first and allow the bias to stretch to the outside.

Basic numbers: A 1″-wide strip makes a ⁵⁄₁₆″-wide stem; a ⅞″-wide strip makes a ¼″-wide stem; and a ¾″-wide strip makes a ³⁄₁₆″-wide stem.

1. With the wrong side of the fabric facing up, fold a 1″ stem in thirds (left to right [a], right to left [b]). It is now folded right sides out, and you're looking at the wrong side of the stem—the side that goes against the background. Pin once at the top [c].

2. Hold the strip in your left hand. With your right hand, baste the length of the strip. Use a #10 milliner's needle with a strong, nonslippery thread and take ⅛"- to 3⁄16"-long basting stitches.

3. When you need to cut a length off the strip, pin a channel and cut [d]. (The pins keep the basting from coming out until you need to cut off more stem.)

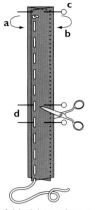

Trifolded, basted stems

4. Place the stem right side up and pin it in place on the background, with one edge just covering the drawn placement line [e]. With this trifold stem, appliqué the inside of a curve first [f]. The other fold will stretch to cover the outside curve. Once both stem sides are appliquéd, pull out the basting stitches [g].

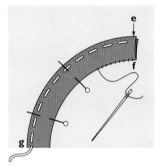

Appliqué inside curve first.

Can a Trifold Stem Finish ⅛" Wide?
Yes. Iron a 1"-wide strip in half, right sides out. Trim the top layer to ⅛" from the fold to the cut edge. Trim the bottom layer to ¼". The ironed fold gives you control to fold this in thirds in your hands. Baste with a #11 milliner's needle and 60-weight cotton thread—use these fine tools so you don't chew up the stem with the basting.

Skinny-Skinny Stems

Inspired by Kathy Dunigan

To make these skinny, quick, trifold silk-ribbon stems, you need a fresh gluestick, a regular round wooden toothpick, and a 7" length of bias-cut silk ribbon, 7⁄16" or 5⁄8" wide (see Sources, page 126). Once you've got the hang of it, you can work up to longer lengths.

1. Cover the underside of the ribbon with glue. The glue dries fast, so complete the following steps quickly.

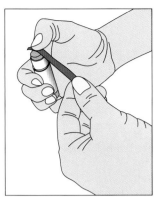

Run the wrong side of the ribbon over the gluestick, holding it down with your thumb, gently (not too much glue) pulling the length across the glue.

2. To fold the ribbon in thirds, hold the ribbon with the glue side facing up, and for the first 1", fold over one-third of the ribbon width, top to bottom, glue side to glue side.

3. Hold the folded end of the ribbon in your left hand with a bit of fold showing, and hold the other end of the ribbon with your right hand. Hold the toothpick (also with your right hand) and starting just inside the initial fold, pull the toothpick along the length of the ribbon, scoring it to make the fold line. Holding the ribbon and toothpick in one hand to make this narrow fold requires practice! For longer lengths, thread the ribbon's tail between your 4th and 5th fingers for control.

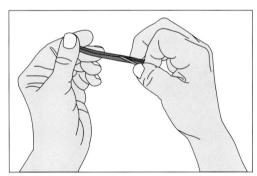

Pull the toothpick along the ribbon's glued side, indenting the first fold line.

4. Repeat Step 1 to glue the underside again. Then repeat Steps 2 and 3 to fold the remaining side. The remaining third of the ribbon should all-but-cover the top third's folded allowance resulting in a Skinny-Skinny Stem.

5. Glue-baste (page 28) the stem in place, and tack stitch (page 29) both sides—ideally with YLI 100 weight silk thread.

Note: Easier yet to make with gluestick, toothpick, and bias-cut silk is page 62's Superfine Stem. Elly enjoys making wreath stems this way. See her examples on page 53 and 54.

Woven Baskets

Basket of Fruit and Flowers (Pattern 23, page 108) by Cate Rosendale

Baskets held blessings in Baltimore's Albums. Our Thanksgiving cornucopia echoes this symbolism. With those folded Stems Made in-Hand (page 62) now part of our repertoire, we can take a quick look at the anatomy of a basket and almost intuitively be able to make the basket in Pattern 13 (page 98). Also intuitive are slat baskets, such as our common bushel baskets.

From Elly's pattern Soulful Thoughts of You made by Linda Goodejohn. Slat baskets are easy with trifold stems and even easier with wired ribbon!

Photo by Linda Goodejohn

THE ANATOMY OF A BASKET

The following baskets have *frames* around a *center window* opening.

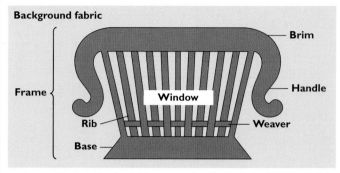

Anatomy of Basket: This basket is woven directly on the background fabric.

Ribs and Weavers

Horizontal and Vertical Weaving

The weavers move horizontally in and out of a basket's ribs. An odd number of ribs means the weavers finish the same on the basket's left and right [c]. Lay out the weavers as you would the strips of a lattice piecrust: First pull back the even-numbered ribs and place a weaver over the remaining odd-numbered ones. Now pull the folded weavers back up. Voilà! Continue odd number, even number, for however many rows you want to weave.

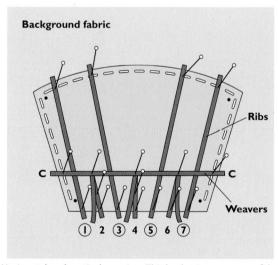

Horizontal and vertical weaving: This basket is woven on a fabric foundation basted to the background.

PIN-PAD TRANSFER METHOD

A pin-pad is simply a pad of lined paper on which you draw your basket, and then pin into your ribs and weavers as you weave them. This method is an easy way to transfer the weaving to fabric, especially when weaving with bias-cut silk ribbon. You can also weave raw-edge bias-cut cotton. Mark bias strips with ¼″ masking tape. After cutting, remove the tape from the fabric, which softens the edge with a touch of fray.

Kathy Dunigan taught me this revolutionary transfer method to use with vertical/horizontal weaving (page 64), or as follows with diagonal weaving.

Window Template Preparation

1. Draw your pinning diagram on a lined pad of paper (the pin-pad).

2. Draw a square. Mark the vertical and horizontal or diagonal center lines.

3. Draw the window for the basket shape and the ¼″ seam allowance beyond.

4. Make a dot for pin-placement (page 68) in each corner, and set aside.

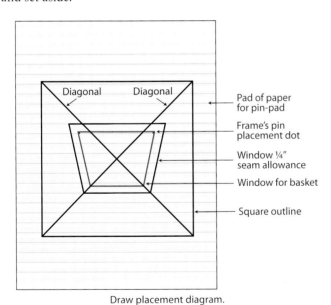

Draw placement diagram.

Diagonal Weaving

1. Cut enough strips to cover the desired basket shape in both directions.

2. Place the ribs on the pin-pad and secure the start of each rib (at the left) with a dot of gluestick applied to the underside with a toothpick—you may have to straighten a

rib, so no globs of glue to regret. Pin the right end of the rib to the pin-pad.

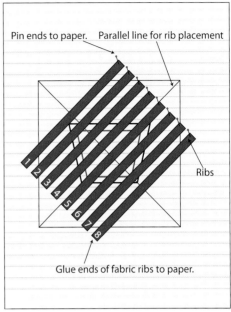

Secure ribs in place.

3. As with horizontal and vertical weaving (page 64), fold back and pin every other rib and place a weaver over the remaining ribs. When you fold back the ribs, secure them with a straight pin to the pin-pad as needed to keep them from shifting.

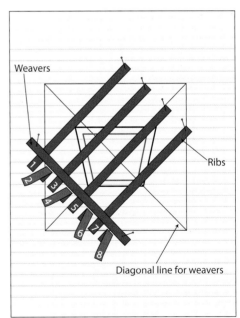

Fold ribs; add weavers.

4. Now pull the folded ribs back up and continue in a similar manner for however many rows you want to weave.

Transfer the Weaving

1. Use an uncut self-stick label sheet, and make a template the size of the window opening of the frame.

2. Remove the protective back of the window template, and tamp the sticky side against cotton or wool to reduce its stick a bit. Place the template on the weaving and draw ¼″ seam allowance all around.

Draw ¼″ seam allowance line.

Uncut self-stick label

Sticky template on top of weaving

3. Seal the ribbon at the ¼″ seam allowance line all around the woven basket with clear nail polish. When dry, cut the weaving ¼″ beyond the window template.

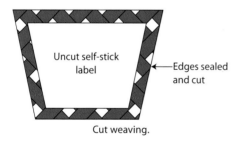

Uncut self-stick label

Edges sealed and cut

Cut weaving.

4. Place the weaving in position on the marked block background using pin placement (page 85). Finely baste using contrasting thread next to the edge of the self-stick label template, attaching the weaving to the background. Gently remove the self-stick label with the help of a toothpick.

5. Prepare the basket frame using Glue Basting with Freezer Paper Shiny Side Up (pages 28 and 30).

6. Smear glue on the turned-under seams of the window. Position the frame over the weaving, using pin placement. Use dabs of glue to hold the outside edges of the basket

frame. After the glue dries, appliqué the inner edge of the basket frame, then the outer edges.

7. To remove the freezer paper template, see page 31.

This basket was woven of Hanah bias-cut ⁷⁄₁₆″ silk ribbon.
Photo by Elly Sienkiewicz

 Tip

To weave Trifold Stems (page 62) of cotton (rather than ribbon), iron the wrong side of the stems with starch and remove the basting. Weave them *wrong side up* on the pin-pad.

Split Leaves

Split leaves are an antique Baltimore style. The look came first from using a striped fabric, often tan on one side and forest green/blue-green moiré on opposite side. Others within the Baltimore community imitated this look by piecing two fabrics down the center vein line. You can machine sew two strips together, iron the seams open, and from this cut ovate leaves. Split leaves add depth and realism to greenery.

Crown of Ruched Roses (Pattern 18, page 103) by Kathy Spielman

Perfect Circles (Perfect Grapes)—Mass Produced!

Grapevine Lyre Wreath (Pattern 17, page 102) by Karen Pessia

By the perfect grape, we mean, of course, a perfect circle. And most often we mean one of the many templated methods—one where the seam allowance of the circle is painted with starch, turned up and over the edge of a circle template, then ironed dry. We had a lively discussion of quicker, newer methods at Quilting in the Tetons 2009. I took down names but lost my notebook, so all that remains are the methods, shared below, with my gratitude.

THE STEADFAST GATHERER CIRCLES

When folklorists write about us quiltmakers 150 years from now, they'll note Karen Kay Buckley's clever Perfect Circles template tool inspired, perhaps, by heat-resistant plastic washers and our own homemade tool. Steadfastly, it gathers to save our stitch time for appliqué. Make yourself one, for history and appliqué!

The Gatherer

1. Use an art store multicircle template with N, S, E, and W registration lines. On the wrong side of fabric, draw a 2″ circle cutting line [a]. Draw centered inside it a 1½″ circle [b], the gather line. Mark the center with a dot [c].

2. Paint the edge [a] with clear nail polish to seal the edge when dry.

3. Use perle cotton 8 (or 5) to stitch a running stitch on [b]. Leave a 6″-long beginning and ending thread. As though to tie your shoes, cross one over the other so they pull against each other (as in tightening your laces).

4. Cut out the circle [a].

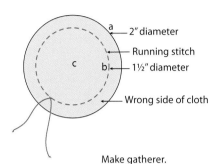

Make gatherer.

The Grape

1. Draw a ¾″ circle Template A on a file folder. Mark the center with a dot.

2. Draw a 1¼″ circle B on the appliqué fabric. Paint just the ¼″ perimeter of the fabric with starch.

3. Cut out A and B. With a toothpick, put a wee spot of gluestick on the back of A. Adhere it, centered, to the wrong side of B.

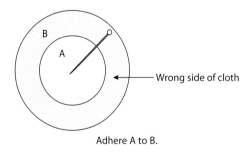

Adhere A to B.

4. Put a pin through the A/B center. Use it to pin-place (page 68) A/B inside the Steadfast Gatherer.

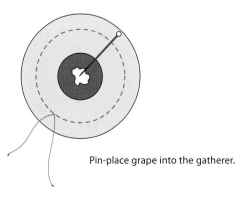

Pin-place grape into the gatherer.

5. Pull the perle cotton until your gatherer is snug over the grape. Pull out the pin, and iron just over the seam edge up to the ruffles until dry. Open up this cloth-wrapped parcel as though it is a gift. This tool can be used over and over. Why not make multiples of these so you can assembly-line gather lots of grapes … and give folks somethin' to talk about!

Iron until dry.

GRAPES IN FOIL

Another so-kind class member offered a method of gathering with a silver tool of aluminum foil, as follows:

1. Cut a ¾″ circle Template A from a file folder.

2. Cut a 1¼″ circle B of fabric. With a toothpick, put a tiny dab of glue at the center of the wrong side of the fabric. Press Template A to this center. Paint starch ¼″ around the perimeter of the fabric.

3. Draw with a black Pigma pen a 2″ circle C on regular-weight aluminum foil. Cut it out. Center A/B on the foil circle C.

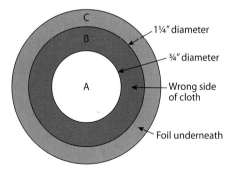

Layered template, cloth, and foil

4. Finger-press the foil up and over until it covers the grape-in-process snugly and smoothly.

5. Iron the seam edge to "broil the grape." Like custard, this recipe calls for leaving the grape in its oven to dry out a bit more. (Foil, after all, keeps things from drying out in the refrigerator.) Open the foil up a bit to let the drying finish.

(Yes, you can use a simple swatch of foil. But then you need to cut back the excess foil to make a chimney for the moisture to escape.)

Broil the grape.

6. Use pin placement (below) to position the grape on the background fabric.

You can appreciate that these broiled (as it were) grapes may be the fastest way yet to make a cookie sheet full of perfect grapes!

NOTE

These two grape techniques work well with the following marking method (also known as pin placement): Mark one dot (a grape's center) on the background fabric. A pin put through the grape center (prick a hole in the template so you can find the exact center from the front) and out into the background will place even a cluster of grapes on the stem.

Quilted Roses

Pulchritudinous roses frolic, in old Baltimore's Albums! Some are top-stitched through the appliqué only. Rarely, padded and quilted, their quilting lines are embroidered—use a stem stitch or chain stitch (pages 56 and 58). I quick-stitch-quilt the lines first, then embroider over them catching the appliqué fabric layer. Scale the thread to the rose size: a single strand of cotton floss, two strands of silk floss, or buttonhole twist, even sewing thread for the smallest flower.

In my experience, antique roses are solids: vivid red or bright white. They are even showier when stencil-shaded by dark purple oil pastel on vivid red fabric (page 48). Stenciling and quilting both begin with the same *perforated* template. Removing (then discarding) a petal template guides one's quilting with no lines drawn. Conversely, the petal template is removed to frame cloth for stencil shading but then is replaced for quilting later. This is a repeat process until, when the rose is shaded, all the petal templates are removed. After you've cut your first perforated template, you'll celebrate this technique's shocking ease!

MAKE A PERFORATED TEMPLATE

A perforated template is one that is not fully cut out, providing the lines needed for marking quilting or stencil shading for oil pastels. The center rose in Pattern 25 is a good place to use this technique.

1. Fold a freezer paper swatch sharply in half, shiny side in. Open it over a lightbox to trace the left half of the rose pattern. Use repositionable tape to hold the freezer paper steady over the pattern.

2. Refold the freezer-paper swatch, and cut systematically:

a. Cut Template 3 (red lines), first from the top, then from the bottom, leaving one full ⅛″ bridge (attachment) uncut. (Follow the red outlines, do not cut on the gap shown between templates 3 and 5.)

b. Next cut Template 4 (blue lines) leaving one full ¹⁄₁₆″ bridge short of the fold on both outlines.

c. Cut the turquoise line between templates 1 and 5, leaving a ⅛″ bridge to be cut through when it's time to quilt it.

d. Cut the red-violet outline of Template 5, starting from the fold at the top, leaving a ¼″ bridge on the side. (Do not cut through the gap shown on the side.) Cut the red-violet outline of Template 1 starting from the fold to the Template 5 bridge.

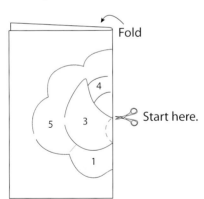

Rose A: Trace pattern and cut.

NOTE

Leaving the rose template attached to the rose window template makes this a multipetal stenciling template. Now that we've learned that, let's continue making this a quilting template by cutting through that last Template 5 bridge, leaving us a quilting template. This makes a perfectly symmetrical perforated template. Handle it gently.

3. Open the rose up and cut (green line) petal 2's dotted line.

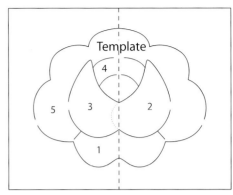

Cut final Template 2 outline out of freezer paper.

PAD, MARK, AND QUILT A ROSE

Padding

1. Trace the outline of the rose template onto the background fabric. (This line confines the padded rose to its intended footprint, though filled with padding.)

2. With an ultrafine Sharpie or other permanent pen, draw the rose outline on Hobbs Thermore Ultrathin Batting.

3. Cut out this batting, ⅛″ *inside* the drawn line, thus keeping it out of the seamline.

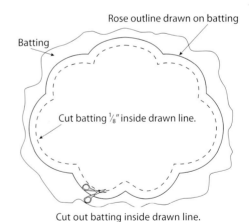

Cut out batting inside drawn line.

3. Dab gluestick on the background at the center of the rose. Adhere the batting rose to the background, pressing it to the gluestick dab.

Marking

1. Iron the perforated rose template (page 70) on the *bias* of the rose fabric, right side up. (The bias augments the loft of the quilted petals.) Mark a ¼″ seam allowance beyond the seamline.

2. Cut out the appliqué along the ¼″ line. *Note:* If you had two or even three layers of batting (each one cut down ⅛″ smaller than the next, like a tiered wedding cake), you would need a bit wider seam allowance to allow for added loft.

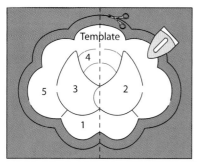

Iron and cut appliqué.

3. Pin-place (page 85) the appliqué over the drawn background line. Pin, then baste through the appliqué, padding, and background.

Appliqué and Quilting

1. With the paper template pressed on tightly, appliqué the outside of the rose. How to avoid the sugar cookie look? A one-layer flower shape can easily soften as though it has risen in the oven. The recipe secret is: Appliqué your best defined inside corners, cutting through the drawn line at the V, but not beyond it (page 30). Savor making your most poetically rolling hill-like outside curves (page 33). Soft hills and steep valleys are the nature of this pattern. Emphasize them.

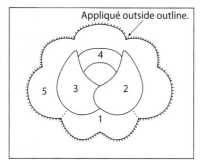

Appliqué outline of rose.

NOTE

You can cut the seam down to taste, after confirming that the seam covers the line and allows for the padding loft (without background distortion). The magic of paper-templated (not drawn) appliqué is that if you need a wider seam allowance for the loft, you have it without any preconceived pattern line drawn for posterity to see.

2. Then, with a color-matched thread, such as YLI Silk 100, quilt petal 1. The edge of the paper template alone marks the quilting. When petal 1 is quilted, cut the petal 1 template free and discard it. Quilt each petal, moving from 2 to 3 to 4. Petal 5 has been quilted as you quilt the adjacent petals: Remove its template also. Petal 5 also quilts petal 1.

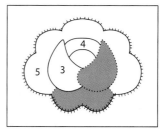

Quilt each petal.

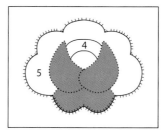 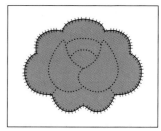

3. Look coldly at your rose. If it looks lovely, you have "the touch." If you are not quite satisfied, embroider a stem or chain stitch (pages 58 and 56) over your quilting and hug it up to the appliqué lines.

Quilted Roses by Jayne Slovick, padded, quilted with the aid of a perforated template, and heavily embroidered inside and around the edge. *Photo by Teri Young*

Baltimore Clipper (Pattern 25, page 110) by Evelyn Crovo Hall. *Photo by Teri Young*

I couldn't resist illustrating a quilted rose as a stencil-shaded rose, or echoing Evelyn Crovo Hall's rose center embroidery. Her two-strand floss pistil stitches or legged colonial knots stand up at the back, all in a row, surrounding a central crowd of clustered colonial knots. It is dramatic even at some distance. This garland sits beneath an exuberant print-cloth sea, no better stylization in appliqué of the mighty ocean. Above this roiling sea, the *Ensure,* her steel-gray sails, pastel-edged batik, puffed out in peaceful perfection, sails in stately grandeur. Flags above, flowers below, we are pulled to study this piece of needleart and we linger on its embellishment details.

Some details, like the stem-stitched spray tossing colonial knot bubbles, playing and laughing, make us smile. Some embroidered embellishment, such as the lazy daisy leaf-edging, is effective because like the row of pistil stitches it is rhythmical and repeated. And are these not essential elements in all good quilt design? Each of us is listening to an inner muse as we appliqué. We're making choices, often unconsciously. I drew the original garland pattern—I liked that big bud to the left of the rose. Like the exuberance of that bursting bud, Evelyn chose instead to use a simple ovate calyx/bud and to make it of an aqua color carried through elsewhere in her garland. I like her choice better than my own. I suspect she came intentionally to carry a shade of the water's blue up to a high-flying flag, and down to the garland below. By such small details we put ourselves into our art. Others will see us in it and know important things about us that perhaps even we do not know. Your way, as we appliquérs say, is the best way.

Double-Sided Fabric Flowers

by Anne Carter

Below are the instructions for making the flowers in Basket of Flowers (Pattern 13, page 98).

Basket of Flowers (Pattern 13, page 98) by Anne Carter

PREPARATION

1. Place 2 pieces of flower fabrics with wrong sides together. Place a piece of Peel*n*Stick fabric fuse sheet on top, with backings still intact. (This product functions like double-sided tape.) Place the template on top of the stack and cut all layers directly on the cutting line of the template.

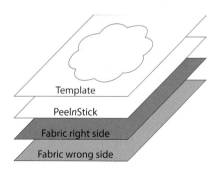

2. Remove the paper liner of the Peel*n*Stick sheet and press the sticky side to the wrong side of the bottom piece of fabric.

3. Remove the remaining paper backing from the Peel*n*Stick sheet, and place it on the wrong side of the remaining fabric piece. A double-sided unit results with right sides showing on both sides.

MAKE THE DOMINANT FLOWER

1. Follow Steps 1–3 above using Pattern B (page 73) for the template.

2. Fold the double-sided fabric unit in half. Use the dotted lines on Pattern B for the remaining fold lines as a guide and bend and fold the fabric in an accordion fashion. Remove the template.

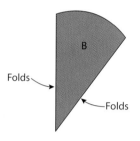

3. Bend the pointed tip of the fabric about ⅜″ from the end; baste folded tip if desired.

4. Holding the folded tip firmly, open up the flower by fanning out the petals. Lay it flat and arrange folds to your liking.

5. Prepare a center circle piece by preparing another double-sided unit in another color using Pattern C (page 73).

6. Tack the center to the flower.

7. Appliqué in place.

MAKE THE SMALLER TRUMPET-SHAPED FLOWER

1. Follow Steps 1–3 in Preparation (page 72) using Pattern D (below) for the template.

2. Fold the body section along the 2 dotted lines toward the back to create creases. Remove the template.

3. Cut an additional piece of Peel*n*Stick using the left, shaded side of Pattern D. Remove the paper backing from 1 side and place the Peel*n*Stick on the left side of the fabric. (Use the shaded side of Pattern D for a guide.)

4. Remove the remaining paper backing from the Peel*n*Stick shape and fold this section toward the back. Bring both sides of the fabric to the back, overlapping the 2 seams as they stick together from the Peel*n*Stick.

5. Turn under about ¼″ on the top of the cone to create a rim around the top edge of the flower. Stitch in place.

6. Create a stamen for the flower from a small piece of pipe cleaner. Make a small loop at each end, place it into the cone, and secure it in place without catching the front of the flower.

7. Appliqué in place.

Yo-Yo Roses

Crossed Stems with Yo-Yo Roses (Pattern 4, page 89) by Connie Chapman.

1. Cut a fabric circle using Pattern A (page 74) for a ¾″-diameter yo-yo.

2. Turn a ¼″ hem to the wrong side. With a running stitch midway between the fold and the raw edge, make ¼″ pleats (2–3 at a time). Pull to gather them until you come full circle. Continue to stitch back through the first 3 pleats, then secure the thread.

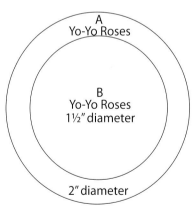

A
Yo-Yo Roses

B
Yo-Yo Roses
1½″ diameter

2″ diameter

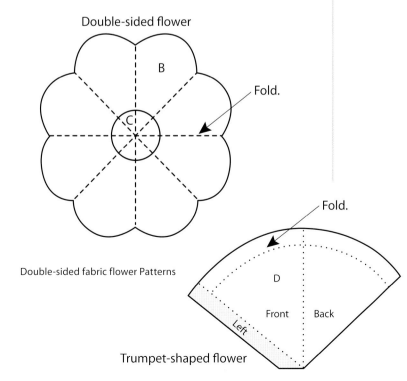

Double-sided flower

B

C

Fold.

Double-sided fabric flower Patterns

Fold.

D

Front Back

Left

Trumpet-shaped flower

Mrs. Numsen's Fringed Centers

To add fringe the center of a yo-yo, cut a fabric circle using Circle Pattern B (page 73). Fringe the circle by pulling threads out of the edge with a needle and tweezers. Fold the circle into eights. Use embroidery scissors to tuck the circle down into a yo-yo.

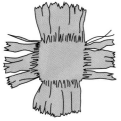

Full circle, fringed

Half circle

Quarter circle

Eighth of a circle

Tuck fringed circle into yo-yo.

Bette's ⅝"-diameter yo-yo flower

Note: The 1½" circle Pattern B also makes ⅝"-diameter yo-yos.

Family Tree House block (Pattern 5, page 90) by Bette Augustine, using 3 layers of Mrs. Numsen's Fringed Centers. *Photo by Bette Augustine*

Fringed Roses
by Bette Augustine

THE FRINGED CIRCLE

1. Cut a 1" × 5" strip on the grain. Fold it in half lengthwise, right sides together.

2. Running stitch the fold close to the edge between [a] and [b]. Pull to gather. Stitch [a] to [b]. Secure the stitches.

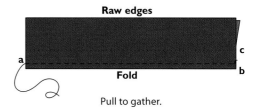

Pull to gather.

3. Use tweezers to pull the threads to fringe between the raw edge and a line [c] ⅛" above the gathering line.

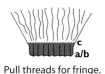

Pull threads for fringe.

4. Flatten the gathered circle and tackstitch the intact fabric ring [d] to the background where you want to place the fringed rose.

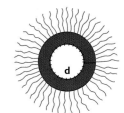

Flatten circle.

Crown of Ruched Roses (Pattern 18, page 103) by Elly Sienkiewicz. This block dances with straight-stitch edge-embroidery (page 60), split leaves (page 66), top-stitched veins (page 55), rose moss embroidery (page 59), yo-yo centers with fringe, colonial knot centers (page 57), and a Rolled Rose center (lower right) taught on page 75. *Photo by Teri Young*

Rolled Rose Center

1. Cut a bias strip 1″ × 4″. Fold it in half lengthwise. Sew a running stitch as close to the raw edges as you can, catching the right corner in the gather line (this will become the rose center [a]).

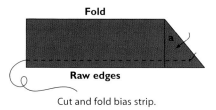

Fold

Raw edges

Cut and fold bias strip.

2. Pull to gather the strip.

Pull to gather.

3. Roll the raw edge into a flower shape fitted to the center of your fringed circle. Hide the end underneath and tack it on the underside to hold its shape.

Roll.

4. Stitch the rolled rose shape into the center of the circle. Bette notes that it should be loose (not gathered so tightly as to stand up stiffly) along its outside edge to create a flower center.

Fringed Rose

Bette Augustine's Very Fancy Flowers

by Bette Augustine

Detail from Rose of Sharon III (Pattern 2, page 87) by Bette Augustine (complete block on page 78)

The following are the instructions to make the dimensional Rose of Sharon flowers such as those shown in Rose of Sharon III (Pattern 2, page 87).

1. Mark the outline of the flower petals on the background fabric.

2. Cut a bias strip of flower fabric 7½″ × 1″. Press under ⅛″ along one long raw edge, wrong sides together (optional: baste edge under). Stitch a basted running stitch ¼″ from the other long raw edge.

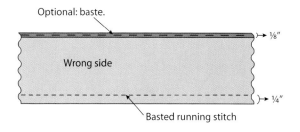

Optional: baste.

Wrong side

⅛″

¼″

Basted running stitch

3. Leave about ½″ of the beginning of the strip free from stitching and pin the end in place. Begin appliquéing the turned under edge along the marked flower petal line.

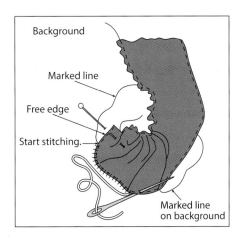

Background

Marked line

Free edge

Start stitching.

Marked line on background

4. Continue stitching around the petal edge, gathering the inner edges as you go. Use a stiletto to help control the fullness. Stitch until you meet up with the beginning stitches. There is plenty of length left in your strip at this point.

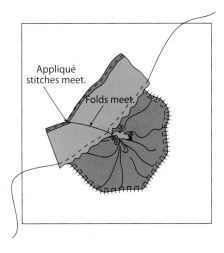

Appliqué stitches meet.

Folds meet.

5. With a stiletto tuck the starting edge of the strip under the other end. Fold the final end of the strip back, where the appliqué stitches meet up. Measure ½″ from the fold line and draw a line crosswise. Undo the basted running stitch at the tail end of the strip so you can trim the end to ½″ without clipping the running stitch. Trim on the drawn line.

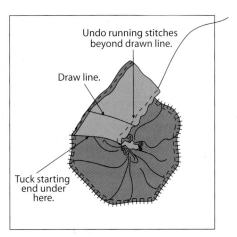

Undo running stitches beyond drawn line.

Draw line.

Tuck starting end under here.

6. Fold the ½″ trimmed edge under. Lay the folded edge flat.

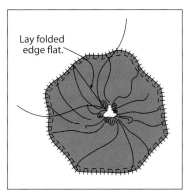

Lay folded edge flat.

7. Pull the gathering thread up and distribute the folds evenly around the petals. Tighten or loosen the stitches per your taste, and knot.

8. Gently remove your basting stitches from the outside of the flower petals.

9. Cover the raw edges of the inside of your flower with your favorite technique for a circle and/or fill with beads or French knots as desired.

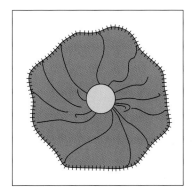

NOTE

If you find that you have too much bulk in the center of the flower, pull out the gathering stitches and add another row of gathering stitches ½″ or so from the raw edge. Trim away about ¼″ along the raw edge, pull up your gathers again, and adjust.

Folded Fabric Rosebuds

Rake Ruched Rose of Sharon (Pattern 9, page 94) by Carrie Thompson

1. Draw Pattern B (below) on the right side of your fabric. Cut it out, adding ⅛″ beyond the circle [a]. Fold the fabric in half. Mark the center of the fold with a pin [b].

2. To reduce the bulk, cut off the top layer ⅜″ below the fold.

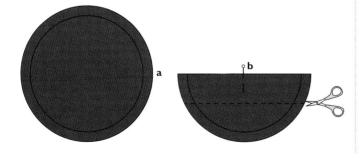

3. Fold from left to right [c], then move over ⅛″ and fold from right to left [d]. Pin to hold [e].

4. Use a running stitch along the drawn line and pull to gather—but just a little! Secure the stitches when the bud's width (at a–b) is ⅞″ [f].

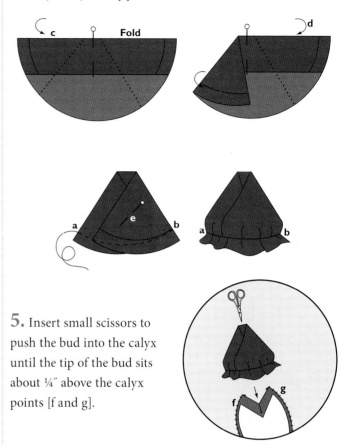

5. Insert small scissors to push the bud into the calyx until the tip of the bud sits about ¼″ above the calyx points [f and g].

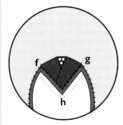

6. Tuck under the calyx seam allowance and appliqué the seam to the top layer of the rosebud [h].

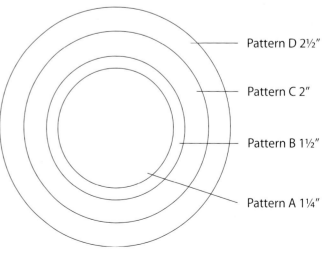

Pattern D 2½″

Pattern C 2″

Pattern B 1½″

Pattern A 1¼″

Patterns include seam allowance

Dual Fabric Rosebuds

Inspired by Bette Augustine

Rose of Sharon III (Pattern 2, page 87) by Bette Augustine.

How did she do it? Mysterious … but so easy!

To make 4, cut 4 freezer-paper bud templates from Pattern 2 (page 87). Add no seam allowances.

Cut 2 strips of fabric as follows:

    Strip A: 1¼″ × 7″ (bottom of the bud)

    Strip B: 1¼″ × 7″ (top of the bud)

1. With right sides together, pin Strip B over Strip A.

2. Using a running stitch, sew a ¼″ seam across the long ends, joining both strips. Begin and end with 6″ thread tails.

3. Pull the threads to gather the seam from a 7″ length down to 5″. Lock the gathering threads with a knot at each end.

4. Press the seam open.

5. Pin (using 2 appliqué pins) the 4 freezer-paper bud templates, shiny side up, onto unit A/B, side by side, leaving room for seam allowances. With clear nail polish, seal the gathering threads between templates.

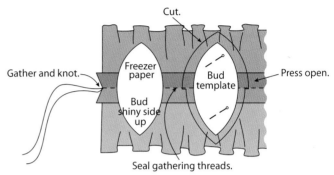

6. Cut out each bud, with a ³⁄₁₆″ seam allowance outside the top of the template, and a scant ⅛″ seam allowance outside the bottom. Clip ¾ of the seam allowance on each side, just above the seamline. Glue-baste (page 28), or heat-baste (page 29) the bud tip seam to the freezer paper above the seamline.

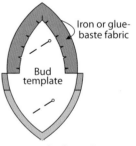

7. Slip the templated bud into the calyx. Pin the top and the bottom of each bud. Appliqué the bud's top seam. Remove the pins.

8. Pull out the paper template with hemostats. Tuck the bud back under the calyx. Pin. Appliqué all edges of the calyx. Repeat for all buds.

Shell Ruching in Fabric

1. Iron a 1″ × 22″ strip of lightweight bias fabric in half lengthwise, right sides out.

2. Mark the seam allowance with a dot [a] ¼″ from the right end. To the left of this dot, mark tiny, unobtrusive dots along the fold every 1″. These dots are the peaks of the mountain stitching pattern.

3. On the bottom edge, mark every 1″, beginning ¾″ from the edge. These are the valleys.

4. Thread a #10 milliner's needle with 20″ of knotted, color-matched, nonslippery thread. Begin below the seam allowance dot and loop the thread over the edge [a], taking ¹⁄₁₆″ running stitches from right to left in a mountain/valley pattern. Throw the thread over whenever you come to the edge. (This loop scallops the edge.) Be careful not to sew through previous stitches—that would prevent gathering.

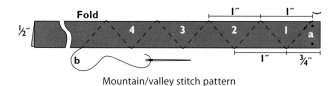

Mountain/valley stitch pattern

5. Stitch 4 complete triangles on the top edge, then pull to gather [b]. Pull tightly enough to form 3½ petals per inch. If desired, shape the petals by pushing them up with embroidery scissors from behind and finger-pressing the perfect petal. Secure the thread before stitching and then gather 4 more triangles. Note that when you pull to gather, the petals puff up, but the thread of the zigzag stitching pattern becomes an almost straight line of stitches dividing the outer (top) petals from the inner petals!

6. Ruche 25 petals and park the needle [Needle A]. If, after shaping the initial rose, you need to ruche more to finish the flower, do so at this time.

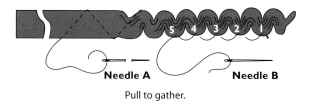

Pull to gather.

7. To form a 5-petal center, stitch together the first 5 petals on the bottom [c]. Pull the thread [Needle B] taut to gather these into a 5-petal center. Secure the thread to lock these in place, but don't cut it. Hold the 5 petals upright, with the ¼″ seam allowance tucked down behind them. Pull up the gathering thread behind the outer row of petals [d] and over to wrap around the juncture between petal 5 and petal 6 three times. Then lock off the thread again, but don't cut it.

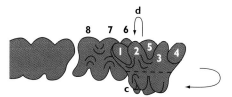

Form 5-petal center.

8. Open this 5-petal center so it lies flat on the next row of petals. The object is to stitch the outside of a center petal to the gathering line of the petal behind it. After you finish the center, the next row becomes the inner row. Stitch the petals to the center stitch line of the outer row until you have just a few petals left. Tuck the tail of the last petal under the rose and tack it to stay. After embellishing the center, appliqué the outer row of rose petals to the background.

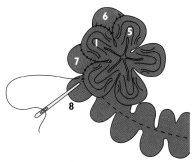

Open center flat and stitch to next row.

9. One way to finish the rose is to simply embroider a ½″ circle full of colonial knots (page 57) using 5-strand floss with 1 wrap. Alternatively, use a yellow ½″ circle center or try centers that are encircled with colonial knots.

Finished shell ruched rose

Star Ruched Rose

A quilter graciously sent me a template shape for ruching done in the shape of a star, but she did not include her name. The star shape ruches magically, and Pattern 12 (page 97) is a perfect place for it to bloom.

1. Trace star Pattern A or B (this page) onto fabric. Cut them out on the outside drawn line.

2. Start with a knot and sew a running stitch [c] and [b], but leave long threads for gathering.

3. Sew a running stitch [a] and pull to gather until 6 even petals are formed. The circle edge will have turned under to form a roughly ⅛″ seam allowance. Secure and then cut the thread.

4. Gather circle [b], then [c]. When the center flattens, secure and then cut the threads.

5. Arrange the petals, pin, baste, and then appliqué the star rose to the background.

Note: Optionally, you could embroider French knots in the center.

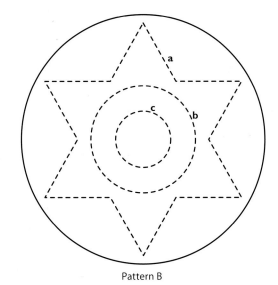

Pattern B

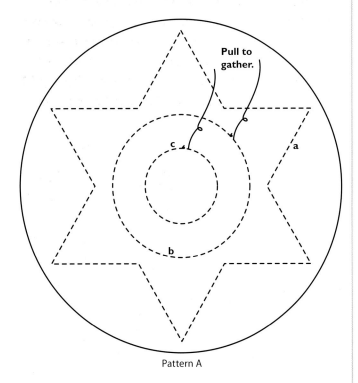

Pattern A

Detail from Star Ruched Rose (Pattern 12, page 97) by Elly Sienkieiwicz. Embellishments include colonial knots (page 57) in variegated thread— yellows and whites, stitched in a crescent to imply perspective. Elly enjoyed applying ink embellishments (page 51), so easy and effective—a quick way to "stitch" the leaves. *Photo by Teri Young*

NOTE

The DVD Elly Sienkiewicz Teaches Advanced Baltimore Appliqué *shows how to make the Star Ruched Rose and more (see Sources, page 126).*

Ribbon Flowers

Ribbon Appliqué bloomed early in the twentieth century, and again at the turn to the twenty-first century.

SHELL RUCHING IN RIBBON

1. For small-scale ribbon ruching, use a ⅝″-wide French shaded wire-edged ribbon. Cut the ribbon 22″ long. Remove the bottom wire.

2. Leave ¾″ between mountain points on the top and between valleys on the bottom to net 3½ gathered petals per inch.

3. Use the same technique as for the 5-petal rose center (Step 7 of Shell Ruching in Fabric, page 79) to make the center, but only use the first three bottom petals. Thread-wrap the juncture between petals 3 and 4. Hold the ruched ribbon strip with the light-colored edge on top, then twist it so the dark-colored edge is on top.

4. To finish, fold forward the 3 center petals, tack them together at the corners, and fill them with colonial knots—5-strand floss, 1 wrap (page 57).

Trifold center ruched ribbon rose by Elly Sienkiewicz

SHOWY RUCHED RIBBON ROSES

The Showy Ruched Rose "happened" in my fingertips and is among the many roses featured in my *Romancing Ribbons into Flowers,* long out of print. Let's look at how to make them, their buds, and embroidered leaves before we take on a potpourri of final fancy embellishments!

As needleworkers, we pass the culture on: the designs, the symbols, the methodology, and where known, the nomenclature. Some of us are faithful reproductionists. Others blend tradition with the stuff of their own lives. Sometimes you can spot a unique needleart thread and trace it from ancient to modern. As my own shell ruching progressed, I folded shaded ribbon ⅛″ off-center, creating a contrasting border that outlines each ruched petal.

In fact, this beauty is full of choices! If you make a ruched rose from an even wider ribbon length, the distance from the center to the first outer row of petals will be longer. If you fold the ribbon length exactly in half, and then mountain/valley ruche, your flower will resemble a carnation, chrysanthemum, or dahlia. If you shorten the cut and crinkle the ribbon in your palm, the ruched flower will look like sailor's britches, bachelor's buttons, pinks, alyssum, or Indian paintbrush.

Showy ruching follows the same procedure as shell ruching (at left) except that initially and for the entire length, the shaded wired ribbon is folded just off-center so that a scant ⅛″ shows of the back ribbon. This botanical wonder shows the coin of our times, for it can only be done in the fine French wire-edged ribbon (see Sources, page 126), much now discontinued. The color of the front layer dominates the rose. The back edge adds the fascination! Leave the wires in—it shapes the petals and allows you to fold the front layer (pale) in half, giving a whole other look. Innovate. Try it on the center petals.

Showy Ruched Ribbon Roses by Robyn MacKay (detail of Clipper Ship, Pattern 25, page 110; full block on page 57). "Showy ruching" formed the first 2½ rows, the shaded ribbon's pale side dominating. Robyn then switched (twisted) to frame the rose, dramatically dark side up!

Photo by Robyn MacKay

Bead Embroidery

To embroider something is to embellish it. Beads are an exquisite ornamentation that adds shine, texture, dimension, and all-around interest to Baltimores. These two specific bead embroidery techniques follow, but in the blocks you'll see many ways of using beads. Remember you can mix and match beading methods as you choose.

SEED BEADS (FLAT)

To stitch a bead flat to the fabric, use a milliner's needle and a strong, fine thread (polyester Nymo would be ideal) color-matched to the bead. Come up through the center of the bead, then over the outside edge of the bead [i]. Then come up in the center again and then over the other side [j].

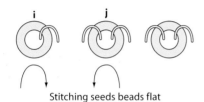
Stitching seeds beads flat

BEADS IN A ROW

Tiny seed beads, row-stitched on end, are often representational (including roses) beginning with an outline, then filling in with concentric lines. A distinctive look, these beads can outline appliqué edges (like a ship's gunnel) or create floral centers. For this embellishment, use strong thread such as Nymo (waxed nylon thread), end-knotted, and a #10 or #11 milliner's needle.

1. Bring your needle up from the back of the fabric, leaving the knot beneath, and thread three beads on it.

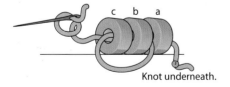
Knot underneath.

2. Backstitch down through the fabric and come up behind [b], then pass through [b] and [c], and out again.

3. Thread on one more bead. Backstitch down through the fabric and come up behind [c], then pass through [c] and [d], and out again.

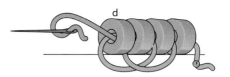

4. Thread on one more bead, and repeat until finished. Lock off with a French knot (page 56) through the last stitch on the back. For insurance: Every few inches, secure your stitches with a French knot on the back or with a dab of clear nail polish.

French knot secures stitches.

Detail from Peacock Pastorale (Pattern 14, page 99) by Elly Sienkiewicz. Seed beads (flat)—Elegant Japanese Delica beads outline the peacock's crown feathers and the ultrasuede on ultrasuede (page 61) butterfly's wings. Between the bird and butterfly, are colonial knots (page 57) and bugle beads with seed bead finishes, as though the pistil-stitch beaded.
Photo by Teri Young

Beads in a row create the red strung-looking beaded "eye feathers" or paisley-like loops on the red wing. Notice the nubby bark that is silk ribbon embroidered. Some is satin stitch (page 58), some, like the two left-most stems are done by the pierced leaf stitch in silk ribbon, as are some leaves.
Photo by Teri Young

All patterns needed for *Happiness Is in the Journey* (pictured on page 12) are yours, here. Patterns ascend from simpler to more complex—like warm-ups before a brisk walk! Cutaway Appliqué (page 32), for me, is the quintessential warm-up. It changed my life. Patterns 1–14 contain a motif easily sewn by Cutaway. Pattern 1 is the easiest of these. Separate unit patterns (15–25) follow. Of this latter group, Pattern 16 is the easiest. Like a bow on a package is a border on a quilt, so don't forget the Dogtooth Border (page 40). It is done by an amazingly simple antiquarian technique first taught through the Family History Block (page 96). New to appliqué? Doing the patterns in ascending order will build on skills learned in previous patterns.

By combining Cutaway Appliqué with Baltimore Albums I became an appliqué devotee. There are so many different appliqué methods. To simplify, I've chosen just my favorites—Needleturn and Freezer Paper Inside—to teach in this book. Appliqué prepared by Freezer Paper Inside is a method so simple for leaves and cookie-cutter flowers that it, too, has changed lives. Fused Appliqué is even easier. Fancywork is always an option. Dimensional Appliqué and embellishments, both painterly and threaded, are taught herein. From perfect grapes "cooked in foil" to embroidery instructions, to revolutionary stems and basket-weaving, *Elly Sienkiewicz's Beloved Baltimore Album Quilts* will

inspire you as you stitch. The ladies of Baltimore gifted us. And are we not their daughters? May your mottoes be "One's *own* way is the *best* way" and "Happiness is in the journey."

Each pattern has a number, symbolic meaning, pattern notes, and either a vintage inscription (for inspiration or inscribing) or the question "Why Baltimore's revival?" responded to by the Friendship Album block makers. It is my question, really: Why is the current Baltimore Album revival gathering momentum even as it approaches its fourth decade? History, too, may well ask, considering the original Baltimore Album movement lasted roughly a dozen years in the mid-nineteenth century, why did its revival in the twentieth and twenty-first centuries last decades—with three mini-revivals so far, within those years?

Pattern Transfer: How to Take a Pattern from the Book

PAPERCUTS

To make a complete papercut pattern, follow the directions below.

1. Fold an 8″ × 8″ square of freezer paper (shiny side in) into 4 quadrants. Orient the square so that there is a fold on the left, 2 folds at the top, and raw edges at the right and bottom.

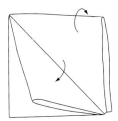

2. Fold down the upper right corners to the lower left corners—the front to the front, the back to the back.

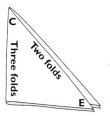

3. You should have 3 folds on the left and 2 folds on the right. Mark the outside edge E and the center C on both the top and the bottom layers.

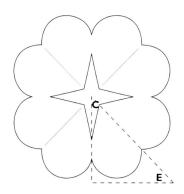

4. If you are making your own papercut, draw your design on the top layer of this 8-layer triangle.

If you are copying a design from this book, unfold the freezer paper and place it shiny side down on the original pattern, orienting the pattern by matching the pattern fold lines and the center (C, where shown) and edge marks (E) to the freezer paper. Use repositionable tape to hold the paper in place over the pattern. Trace an eighth, a quarter, or half of the pattern, depending on the symmetry.

5. Fold the paper and staple inside the appliqué design to keep the layers from shifting. Use excellent paper scissors and cut off the drawn line (so that the pattern's inside corners don't grow, like a sugar cookie in the oven).

CUTAWAY APPLIQUÉ WITH A DRAWN TURN LINE

Use this method to transfer the Cutaway patterns (1–14) to fabric.

1. Cut a 10″ × 10″ square of each of the following: the dominant appliqué fabric, the background fabric, and the freezer paper. Fold each square in fourths—these creases identify the vertical center, the horizontal center, and the pattern center.

2. Set the iron on the Cotton setting and place the appliqué fabric square on a breadboard or other firm surface. Copy or trace the selected pattern onto the paper side of freezer paper, and cut it out along the printed or drawn line.

3. With right sides up, layer the squares so the appliqué fabric is on top of the background fabric. Place the freezer-paper template shiny side down on the right side of the appliqué fabric. Align the template's quadrant folds over the fabric's quadrant creases.

Note: You can also photocopy the pattern onto self-stick uncut label sheets available at an office supply store. Some people use just the paper to signal where the turn line is. If you are a beginner, use a drawn turn line as described below—it will make your inside corners easier.

4. Work on a firm surface like a breadboard: Use a hot, dry iron preheated to the Cotton setting to iron the freezer paper to the fabric.

5. Draw around the freezer-paper template with a Pigma .01 pen or other fabric-marking pen. I prefer a permanent pen that won't run when wet, such as the silver Sakura Gelly Roll, which marks both light and dark fabrics. Remove the freezer-paper template.

6. Prepare the block by pinning the pattern-marked appliqué fabric to the background (see Preparing a Block for Cutaway Appliqué, in Appliqué Basics, page 32).

Prepare block.

SEPARATE UNIT APPLIQUÉ WITH FREEZER PAPER INSIDE

Use this method to transfer individual units in the patterns to fabric.

For Separate Unit Appliqué, you may need to trace or cut the patterns apart. Also, when a pattern is layered so that entire pattern motifs overlap, you'll need to trace those separate elements as separate templates. Follow these steps:

1. Trace the pattern onto the paper side of freezer paper. Alternatively, transfer the pattern by photocopy as follows: Rough-cut the templates out of the photocopy. Paste the copies print side up to the paper side of the freezer paper.

2. Cut out each template, carefully cutting on the printed line.

3. Pin the freezer paper shiny side up to the wrong side of the appliqué fabric. Use 2 small pins.

4. Cut a solid ¼″ seam allowance around the freezer-paper template.

5. Use a fresh gluestick to adhere the seam allowance to the shiny side of the freezer paper. This is the easy alternative to ironing it to the shiny side.

When the appliqué thus templated is sewn, slit the back and pull the paper out with a hemostat or tweezers. Because the glue dries to the shiny side, shift the seam to break the hold, and the paper will come out so easily!

This Freezer Paper Inside template use requires simple skills for curves, points, and inside corners. Refer to Prepared Appliqué with Freezer Paper Inside (page 29) for further information.

Refer to Placement on the Background (below) for methods of placing the appliqués on your block.

Placement on the Background

MARKING THE BACKGROUND FABRIC FOR PLACEMENT OF SEPARATE UNIT APPLIQUÉ PIECES

1. Photocopy the pattern and place it right side up over a lightbox.

2. Center the background and pin it right side up on the pattern.

3. Use a fine pencil or permanent pen (Pigma or silver Sakura Gelly Roll) to trace the pattern 1/16″ inside the printed appliqués onto the background. Iron to heat set. When appliquéing, use Pin Placement (at right) to make sure the drawn line is covered.

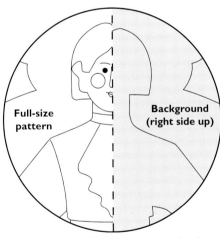

Trace pattern 1/16″ inside printed appliqué.

I prefer marking the right side of the background with the full pattern for complex Separate Unit Appliqués.

MINIMAL MARKING AND PIN PLACEMENT FOR POSITIONING

Minimal marking is a technique you can use if you don't enjoy the fixed attention required to make sure the drawn line is always covered as you stitch. The goal is to make small, recognizable marks that specify placement. Avoid something that looks like a confusing mass of dots and squiggles!

Minimal marking is a bit like code or shorthand, and you can make up your own. For example, I use a dot • to mark the center of a circle when marking for grape appliqués. For leaves, I put an arrow 1/16″ inside each point and a dot at the base, and join them using a straight line representing the center vein: ←•. Similarly, use dots to mark floral placement by putting a dot on the background fabric at each alignment point of the flower shape. Use natural alignment points on the appliqué shapes such as corners, centers, or edges.

To make sure the appliqué is well placed, put a pin through the appliqué and through the marking into the background.

USING A LIGHTBOX

Here is another easy method for accurate pattern placement. Try placing a pattern over a lightbox, then returning to the lightbox as needed for pinning Separate Unit Appliqué shapes in place on the background fabric. Or try using a lightbox to position and pin or glue-baste all the shapes in a block.

Enlargement Percentages for Larger Album Block Sizes

The patterns in this book are presented for an 8″ × 8″ finished block. If you prefer to make larger blocks and quilts in the classic Baltimore Album style, the simplest way is to use a photocopier to enlarge these blocks.

Current design area: 7″ on an 8½″ square (includes ¼″ seam allowance all around) makes an 8″ block, finished. The 12½″ unfinished block size is that of the *Baltimore Beauties* series.

For a 10″ finished block, enlarge 129% (9″ design area).

For a 12″ finished block, enlarge 165% (11½″ design area).

For a 13″ finished block, enlarge 179% (12½″ design area).

For a 14″ finished block, enlarge 186% (13″ design area).

For an 18″ finished block, enlarge 243% (17″ design area).

For a 22″ finished block, enlarge 300% (21″ design area).

ROSES FOR HANS CHRISTIAN ANDERSEN

Symbolism

Roses for love; red rosebuds for youthful, innocent love; crown of roses implies marriage

Why Baltimore's Revival?

In one word—beauty. We all long for, desire, and covet beautiful aspects in our lives. Nothing (to me) is as beautiful as a Baltimore Album Quilt.
—Kathryn Tennyson

Pattern Notes

For the leaf/stem foliage, use Cutaway Appliqué (page 32)—the temporary pattern bridge (page 39) holds the separate stems of this crown in place until the pattern is transferred to fabric. For the folded rosebuds use Pattern C on page 77; optionally, turn the calyxes over freezer paper using glue (page 30). Appliqué just the outside of the calyxes, insert rosebuds (pin in 2 places), and complete the appliqué.

Pattern Notes continue on page 111.

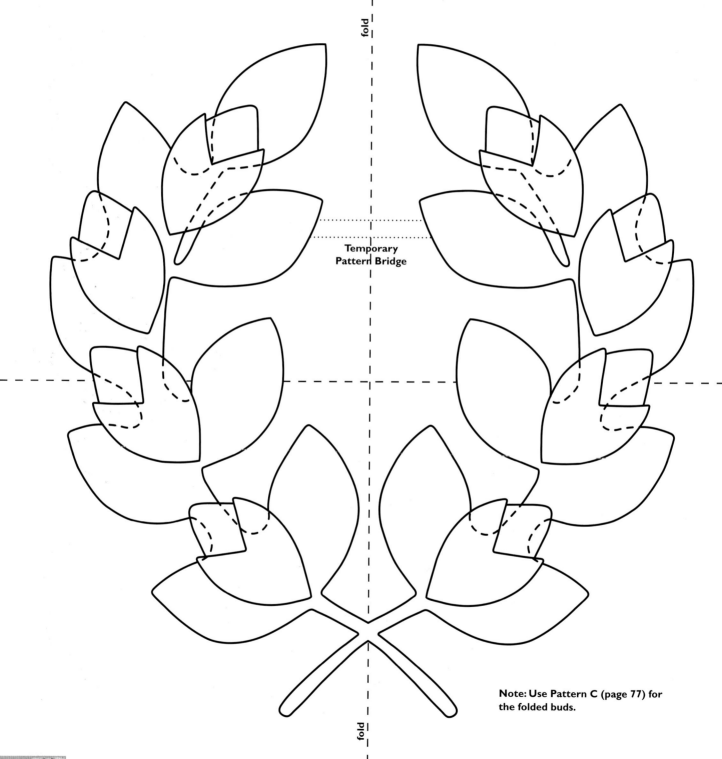

fold

Temporary
Pattern Bridge

fold

Note: Use Pattern C (page 77) for the folded buds.

ROSE OF SHARON III

Symbolism

Wedded love, from the Song of Solomon

Why Baltimore's Revival?

I think it is because it is something that can be created to be very personal. Then it is passed on and it shows what kind of woman one was.

—June Purpura

Pattern Notes

For the foliage use Cutaway Appliqué (page 32). Sew only up to the base of the calyx. Leave the ³⁄₁₆″ seam allowance along all calyx edges cut but not sewn.

Pattern Notes continue on page 111.

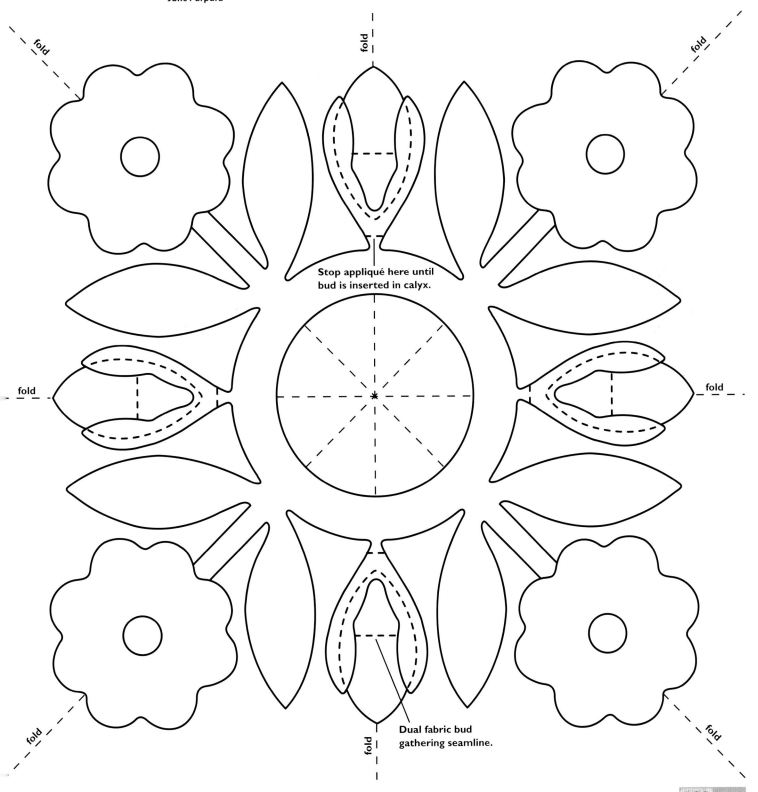

fold

fold

fold

Stop appliqué here until bud is inserted in calyx.

fold

fold

Dual fabric bud gathering seamline.

fold

fold

fold

Fleur-De-Lis with Rosebuds III

Symbolism

Roses for love, the lily for Christ or salvation, the square for moral perfection

Why Baltimore's Revival?

I think people love that they can make blocks their own with their own fabrics and the designs that speak to them…but still be part of a tradition that is centered in the United States.

—Cathy Graves

Pattern Notes

For the foliage use Cutaway Appliqué (page 32) on the inside square. Appliqué the outside of all four calyxes to ½″ below their points. For the rosebuds cut 4 circles, using Pattern D (page 77), fold, and insert the folded bud in place. Complete the calyx appliqué. Optionally, appliqué the rosebuds flat, using Freezer Paper Inside (page 29)—use 2 pins to avoid pivoting, and add ink embellishments (page 43).

Note: Use Pattern D (page 77) for the folded buds.

PATTERN 4 · CROSSED STEMS WITH YO-YO ROSES

Symbolism

Multiflora
rose—grace;
rosebud—beauty,
purity, youth

Why Baltimore's Revival?

*Elly asked me to make one of the diagonal
blocks for what was to become* Through Tufts
of Broidered Flowers. *I was so thrilled to be
asked that I walked around on clouds until I
actually finished the block, mailed it to her,
and started waiting to see how she liked it. By
the time I finished the last of the blocks, I had
learned to take things a bit more calmly.*

—Susan Kurth

Pattern Notes

Trace the left half of the pattern onto an
8″ × 8″ freezer-paper square folded in half.
Cut out the template leaving the temporary
pattern bridge (page 39) in place. Open
up the square and delete Stem A from the
right half. See page 73 for instructions on
making the Yo-Yo Roses. Optionally, add
stem-stitch tendrils (page 56) and Separate
Unit Appliqué leaves (page 31) for contrast,
ink embellishments (page 43), and beaded
flower centers (page 82), or Mrs. Numsen's
Fringed Centers (page 74).

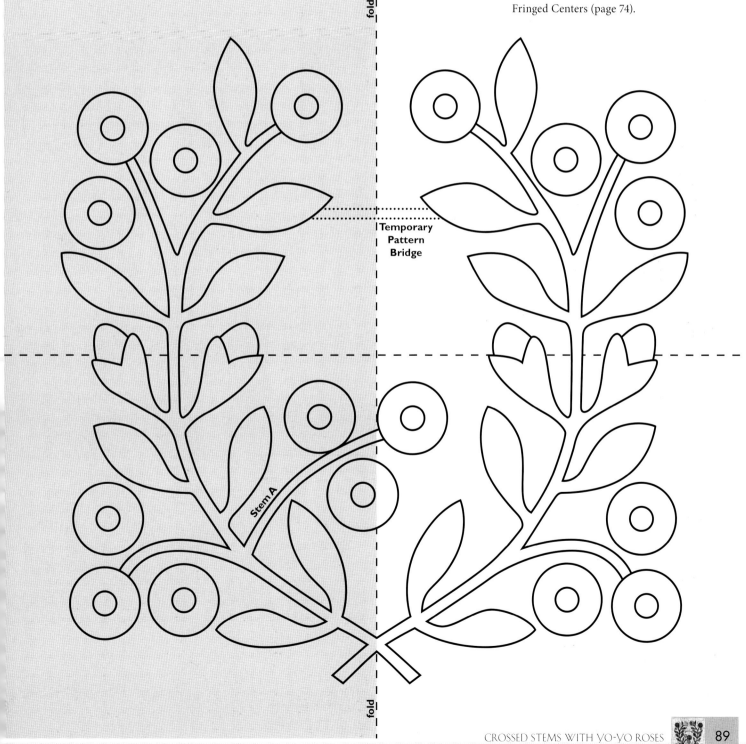

fold

Temporary
Pattern
Bridge

Stem A

fold

fold

FAMILY TREE HOUSE

Symbolism

Birds—life of the soul; bird nest and eggs—new birth, fertility, children

Why Baltimore's Revival?

I believe it's about being a part of history, both the past and creating our own. The original Baltimore Album Quilts represent a unique time of history. To re-create them with the flair of the twenty-first century is challenging and exciting and rewarding.

—Fran Lopes

Pattern Notes

For the tree and foliage use Cutaway Appliqué (page 32). Edge the circles with a row of chain stitch (page 58) using 2 strands of floss and connect the apples to the branches with a double row of chain stitch—use small stitches done in a hoop, tugged slightly to shorten. Hint: Mix 2 colors or shades of floss. Bette Augustine makes a great bird's eye with 1 strand black floss and 1 strand pale mustard in a colonial knot (page 57). Make the bird using Separate Unit Appliqué (page 31). For perfect circles, see page 67 and then add optional ink embellishments (page 43), or try Ultrasuede Appliqué (page 60) or Mrs. Numsen's Fringe Centers (page 74) starting with a 1″ circle.

Katya Sienkiewicz   *Born September 17, 1977!*

SQUIRREL'S BERRY BREAKFAST

Symbolism

Squirrel—thriftiness

Why Baltimore's Revival?

First and foremost, I believe it is the wonderful quilts themselves. Next, modern technology is enabling us to share information more easily, allowing women everywhere to become involved.

—Genia Holland

Pattern Notes

For the branches and foliage use Cutaway Appliqué with a temporary pattern bridge (page 39). For the circles see page 67. For the squirrel use Separate Unit Appliqué (page 31) or try Ultrasuede (page 60). Optionally, add ink embellishments (page 43).

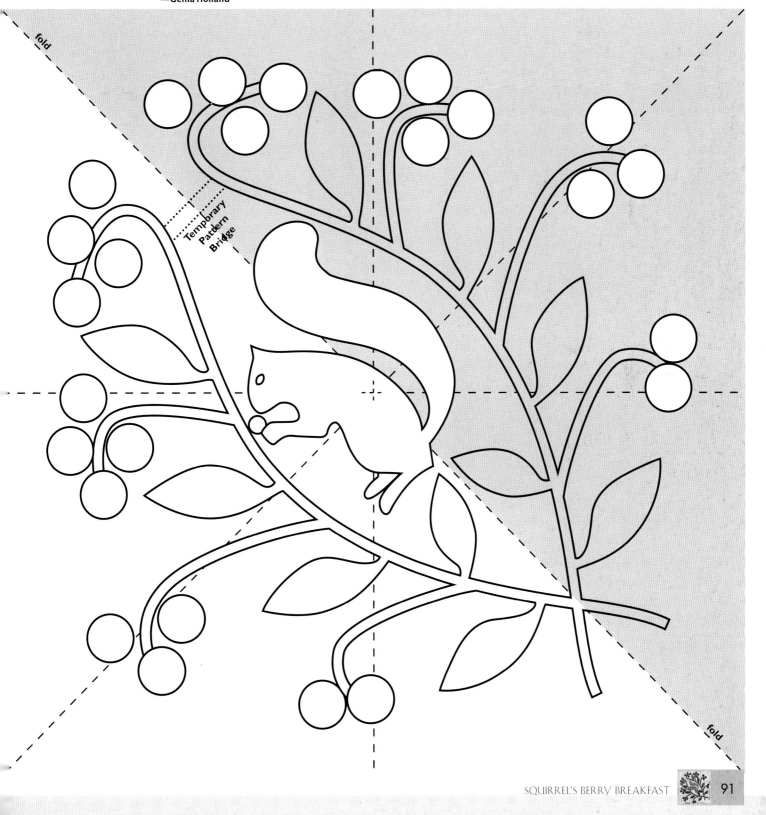

ROSE LYRE II

Symbolism

Lyre for all music in honor of God, eternal music; a red rose means love, and when paired with two red rosebuds, means secrecy; to the poet Robert Herrick, rosebuds meant the fleetingness of life, hinting that this block may be made *in memoriam*.

Vintage Inscription

Let me to the valley go,
This pretty flower to see,
That I may also learn to grow,
In sweet humility.

Pattern Notes

For the foliage use Cutaway Appliqué (page 32). For the lyre, buds, and cookie cutter–like flowers use Needleturn or Freezer Paper Inside (pages 29 and 32). Appliqué the inside of the calyx after the buds are in place (Pattern 2 Notes, page 111). To fold the rosebuds use Pattern B (page 93).

Pattern Notes continue on page 111.

fold

fold

Note: Edge embroidery, whipstitched in original, could be interpreted in blanket stitch.

LYRE WREATH IN BLOOM

Symbolism

Lyre, all music in honor of God; bird, life of the soul; rosebuds, youth or brevity of life; full-blown Rose of Sharon, wedded love

Why Baltimore's Revival?

The most beautiful quilts seem to me to be the Baltimore Album Quilts. The colors and designs, along with the stitches done so lovingly, take the breath away.

—Jo Ann Hudgins

Pattern Notes

1. Cut 1 Pattern A for the lyre wreath—cut double on the fold. Include the temporary pattern bridge.

2. Cut 8 circles from Pattern B (below) for folded rosebuds (page 77).

3. Cut 2 each of Pattern C or cut 2 each of Patterns Ca and Cb for split leaves (below).

4. Cut 1 each of Pattern Da (bird body) and Db (separate wing). Appliqué the head, then draw the beak [Dc] to be satin-stitched (page 58) after appliqué.

Pattern Notes continue on page 111.

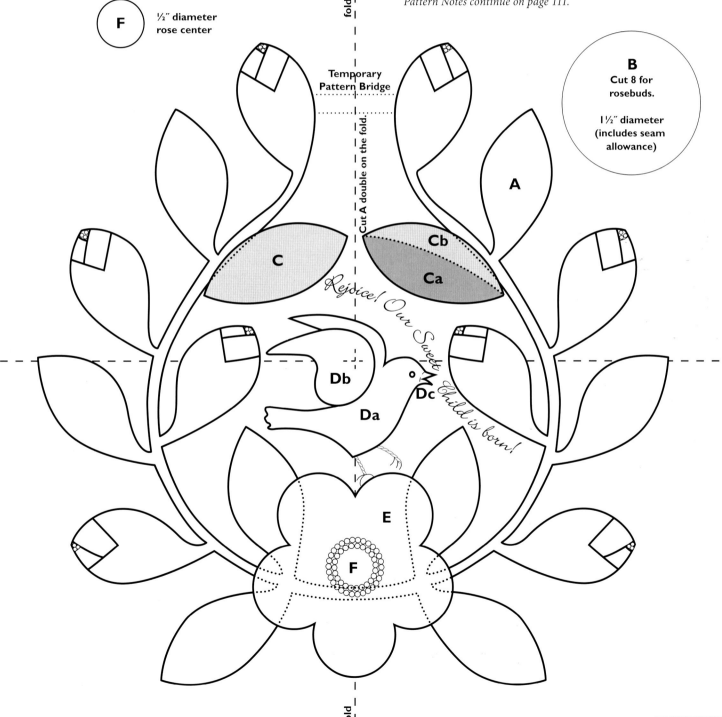

F ½″ diameter rose center

fold

Temporary Pattern Bridge

Cut A double on the fold.

B
Cut 8 for rosebuds.

1½″ diameter (includes seam allowance)

A

Cb

C

Ca

Rejoice! Our Sweet Child is born!

Db

Dc

Da

E

F

fold

RAKE RUCHED ROSE OF SHARON

Symbolism

Rose—love, symbol of Venus, goddess of love

Why Baltimore's Revival?

I think Elly and her books are responsible for much of this revival. She is loved by so many appliquérs, and her fabric lines make up Baltimore Album Quilt blocks so beautifully.

—Joyce Barone

Pattern Notes

For the wreath use Cutaway Appliqué (page 32). For the leaves use Separate Unit Appliqué (page 31), or they can be done by Fusible Appliqué (page 60).

Use Folded Fabric Rosebuds using Pattern A (page 77) and appliqué the insides of the calyxes after the buds are inserted. Use a stem stitch (page 56) to outline the inner circle of the wreath and colonial knots (page 57) at the rosebud tips and at the rose centers. Optionally, use ink embellishments (page 43).

fold

fold

fold

C

B

A

Stem stitch

Above the dotted line, leave the calyxes unbonded until the bud has been inserted.

Use Pattern A (page 77) for the folded buds.

C

fold

fold

fold

fold

E

RUCHED HYACINTH

Symbolism
Hyacinth—peace of mind, prudence, yearning for heaven, unobtrusive loveliness

Why Baltimore's Revival?
The beauty and skill required to make such wonderful quilts and the attempt to bring this beauty into our modern world
—**Jana Vosika**

Pattern Notes
The Ruched Hyacinth [B] is most easily done in ⅞"-wide French shaded wire-edged ribbon*—you need about 5". Shell ruche, 1" from mountain peak to mountain peak (page 79). Needleturn (page 32) the starting end of the ruched strip to the curve of the flowers drawn on the green.

*Can substitute with 1" × 5" bias cotton fabric.

Pattern Notes continue on page 111.

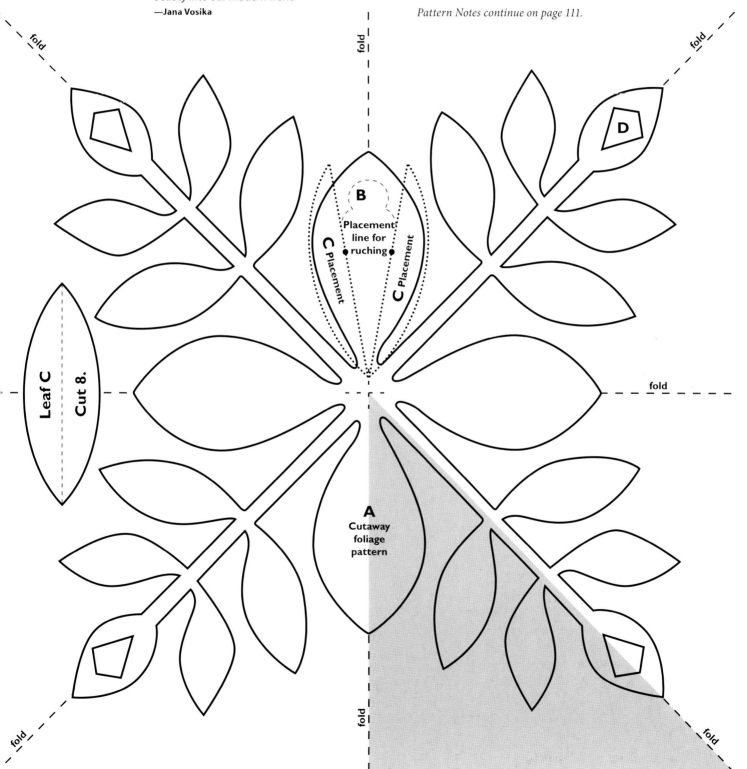

Leaf C

Cut 8.

B

Placement line for ruching

C Placement

C Placement

D

A
Cutaway foliage pattern

fold

FAMILY HISTORY BLOCK

Symbolism

Geometry's square, as a symbol for moral perfection, derives from ancient fraternal Masonry. A circle, without end, is a symbol for immortality. The triangle can represent the trinity when framing the all-seeing eye of God.

Victorian Inscription

Friendships multiply joys and divide griefs.
—Henry George Bohn

Pattern Notes

This block can be most simply appliquéd using Cutaway Appliqué (page 32). But don't miss this opportunity to learn the Dogtooth Border (page 40) on its perimeter! Note: See 8 (dramatic!) repeats of this block in *Happiness Is in the Journey* (page 12). Those blocks showcase pastel portraits of the Sienkiewicz grandparents with six of their grandchildren. Delicate in color, fine in inked detail, their open circle centers still lead the eye to the center medallion. The Photo Silhouette Portraits (page 49), the inking (page 43), and the dynamic easy-fold Dogtooth Border are also taught visually step-by-step on the DVD *Elly Sienkiewicz Teaches Beginning Baltimore Appliqué* (see Sources, page 126).

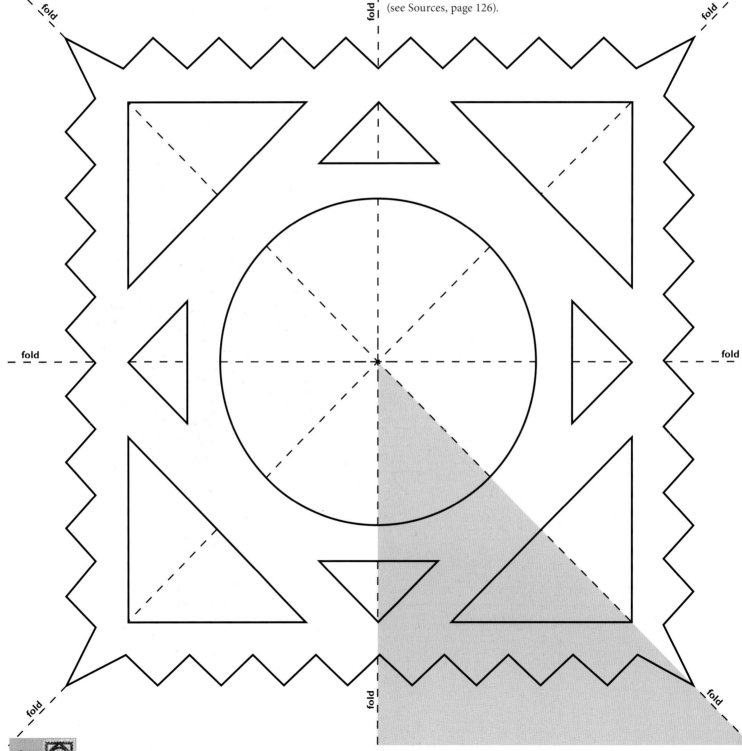

STAR RUCHED ROSE

Symbolism

A star, in general, means divine guidance. Where, you ask, is this pattern's star? It is the gathering pattern! A rose, in general, means love.

Vintage Inscription

When with the needle I'm employed
Or whatsoever I pursue
Teach me O Thou Almighty Lord
To keep my final end in view.
—1809 needlework inscription

Pattern Notes

For the large and medium stems, use a temporary pattern bridge (page 39) that holds the separate stems in place until the pattern is transferred to fabric as follows.

Transfer the main leaf stems to a square of appliqué fabric. Cut the square the same size as the background square. (See page 84 for pattern transfer for Cutaway Appliqué.) Pin the pattern-marked main stem fabric over the background fabric, right sides up. Do the stem by Cutaway Appliqué (page 32). Leave ¼″ under-lap (page 31) everywhere a Star Rose or bud blooms.

Pattern Notes continue on page 112.

Flower B

Temporary
Pattern Bridge

Flower A

fold

BASKET OF FLOWERS

Symbolism

Baskets symbolically contain blessings; flowers are symbolic of spiritual blessings, their perfume (like incense rising from a funerary urn) a sweet soul ascending to heaven.

Why Baltimore's Revival?

I believe these quilts tug at our heartstrings, and when we see them, they speak to us of our past and yet make us look to our future. The enjoyment that the blocks give, as we make each unique in our own way, pulls us to this wonderful artwork.

—Kathy Dunigan

Pattern Notes

Transitional techniques are used here: Some of both the foliage and the basket are patterned separately for Cutaway Appliqué (page 32). Part of this pattern's delight is that it invites your own interpretation. The first time I made it, my basket was a single fabric with only the print's impression of woven stems and weavers. My flowers could well have been lovely, flat, cotton appliqué. French wired-ribbon flowers were irresistible, though!

Pattern Notes continue on page 112.

fold

fold

PEACOCK PASTORALE

Symbolism

The peacock is a symbol of immortality, generally and in Catholic art. The ancients believed peacock flesh did not decay after death. The "eyes" on its tail can represent stars or the "vault of heaven." To Christians (and this would be the primary Baltimorean interpretation), the "hundred eyes" in the peacock's tail are symbols of omniscience, the all-seeing eye of God.

Vintage Inscription

The pride of the peacock is the glory of God.
—William Blake

Pattern Notes

Such elegant advanced appliqué! Take it on easily: Make the tree by Cutaway Appliqué (page 32) or embroider the trunk and limbs by leaf stitch with 4mm silk embroidery ribbon. After the tree is grown, bud it out and invite the peacock to nest there using Separate Unit Appliqué (page 31). Add leaf embellishments using a stem stitch with a French knot (page 56) at the end. For a larger block, use beads. In *Dear Friends Remembered* (page 16), there is even a peahen block.

Pattern Notes continue on page 112.

color p53

BALTIMORE'S ICONIC EAGLE

Symbolism

As symbol, the eagle is ancient and eclectic from uniting the Sun God and the Earth in Native American Culture, to evoking salvation for Christians, and representing pride, protection, and power.

Why Baltimore's Revival?

Women have long been the protectors of civilization's artistic aspects, particularly in times of civil unrest. I think the women then, as now, are attracted to the Baltimore Album Quilts because they recognize this in those works. It helps to give us a sense of our world as it could be. It, too, gives us an opportunity to stitch a statement about ourselves in the hopes that future generations will recognize it.
—Kathleen H. Gordon

Pattern Notes

This glorious advanced block was rendered exquisitely by Sandy Butler (page 56). The colors are vibrant and painted by an artist. Sandy's touch of yellow, stem-stitched onto a bud in sewing thread, is perfect!

Pattern Notes continue on page 112.

ELLY SIENKIEWICZ'S BELOVED BALTIMORE ALBUM QUILTS

ROSE OF SHARON

Symbolism

Rose of Sharon—romantic love, linked with love from the Song of Solomon

Why Baltimore's Revival?

Really so little is known about so many old quilts. I believe we are drawn by the mystery of who these women were and what their lives were like.

—Marla Landt

Pattern Notes

This is an excellent beginning lesson in Separate Unit Appliqué (page 31). Begin with the solid circle drawn on the background. Place the raw edges of a folded Superfine Stem (page 62) to just cover that drawn line. After finely sewing the row of running stitches, pin the stem open every 3″ to appliqué the roses. Fold and place the 4 flowers' rosebuds using Pattern A (page 77), and situate the calyxes over each one. Secure each with 2 pins. Appliqué the calyxes, then close and appliqué the stem. Tack the bud tops down (from the back). Stitch the leaves and flowers by Separate Unit Appliqué. Embroider the concentric ring center with colonial knots (page 57). Optionally, add ink embellishments (page 43). Top-stitching (page 55) the leaves and rose petals would be a lovely finishing touch!

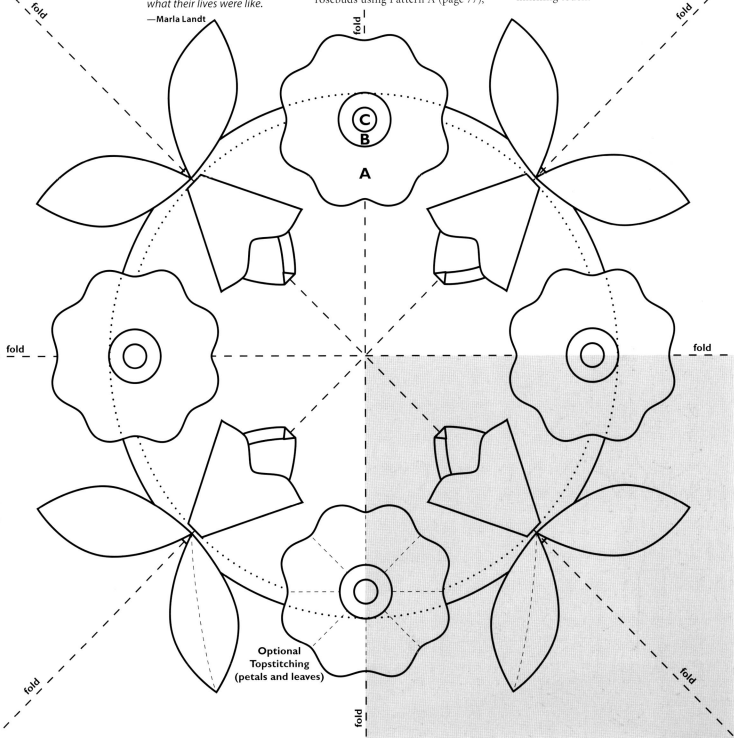

Optional
Topstitching
(petals and leaves)

GRAPEVINE LYRE WREATH

Symbolism

The grapevine is a symbol of abundance and life. In ancient Greece it was a symbol of rebirth as well. For Christians this is reflected in Eucharistic wine: "I am the vine, you are the branches …" John 15:5

Why Baltimore's Revival?

Their beauty and artistry are soul-grabbing.
—Myra Forbyn

Pattern Notes

Draw each stem's *outside* curve line (only) on the background fabric. Make the Superfine Stems (page 62), pressing their prefolded side up and over the running stitches to appliqué along the widest side. Do the leaves next, by Freezer Paper Inside (page 29) or by Needleturn (page 32).

Pattern Notes continue on page 114.

fold

fold

CROWN OF RUCHED ROSES

Symbolism

As a sign of love, ancient Greeks and Romans laid a crown of roses on statues of their deities. Christian women being marched to martyrdom in Rome wore crowns of roses to signify love and their joy at salvation. Mourners collected the cast-off roses and said the rosary; the word *rosary* means crown of roses. The green of a rose stem is a symbol of hope. A crown of roses symbolizes virtue and love and often refers to weddings.

Why Baltimore's Revival?

I think it's the history that is, or can be, captured in these beautiful quilts. They speak so clearly of our American heritage, which has become so very important to us since September 11, 2001. At heart, we miss the gentler way of life.
—**Marsha J. Smith**

Pattern Notes

This is a wonderful block on which to learn or teach ruching and embellishments. Transfer the pattern as for Pattern 17, drawing the dashed rose circles on the background.

Pattern Notes continue on page 114.

PATTERN 19 SPINNING RUCHED ROSES

Symbolism
Roses for love

Vintage Inscription
May this year's roses be
Many and sweet
And few be the thorns
Where wander thy feet.
—1893 needlework inscription

Pattern Notes
Mark the background as for Pattern 17, drawing the dark stem line and the outside of the rose circles. Begin with 2 fine, trifold stems (page 62) pinned, then basted. For the ruched rose, see page 80.

Use Separate Unit Appliqué (page 31) for leaves and yellow petals and use the outline stitch (page 56) to highlight the yellow shapes and for small stems. Colonial knots (page 57) outline the cheerful centers. Optionally, add ink embellishments (page 43).

ELLY SIENKIEWICZ'S BELOVED BALTIMORE ALBUM QUILTS

A HERO'S CROWN (DOVE AND ANCHOR)

Symbolism

The dove is a symbol of the soul and of the Holy Spirit. It signifies peace, gentleness, and purity. The dove in the Albums is an icon of the Rebekahs, the Odd Fellows' Ladies Auxiliary (begun in 1851). A broken wreath is a hero's (just like an Olympic winner's) crown; a dove symbolizes peace or messages; an anchor represents salvation; the bow ties, a "bundle of sticks," symbolic to the Rebekahs of the strength in unity, much like the beehive where unified industry creates a thing of beauty.

Vintage Inscription

Beauty and pride, we often find,
betray the weakness of the mind;
He handsome is and merits praise,
That handsome does, the Proverb says.

Pattern Notes

Begin with the stem, the dove, and the anchor. There has been much hypothesizing about professional artistry in the Baltimores: This block's balance is very sophisticated!

Pattern Notes continue on page 115.

VICTORIAN VASE OF FLOWERS

Symbolism

Like an urn, a vase is a vessel of life of the soul (hence funeral urns); its flowers symbolize the sweet soul ascending to heaven.

Why Baltimore's Revival?

I just know that Baltimore Album Quilts have a uniqueness about them. It doesn't matter, really, how well they are made. It is that beauty and that uniqueness that draws women to want to know more. Curiosity starts so many Baltimore Album Quilt journeys. The more one learns, the more one wants to be a part of the Baltimore Album revival to create her own history and display her own unique character.
—**Robyn MacKay**

Pattern Notes

A most endearing neoclassical vase of flowers, this appears to be one of a kind. The appliqué is quite straightforward and moderately time-consuming. But the embroidery, which really makes this block, visually, will also take considerably longer to do.

Pattern Notes continue on page 115.

LOVEBIRDS IN A WREATH

Symbolism
Lovebirds and parakeets—romantic love

Vintage Inscription
The time of the singing of birds is come, and the voice of the turtle is heard in our land.
—The Song of Solomon

Pattern Notes
Start this block with Superfine Stems (page 62) and use Separate Unit Appliqué (page 31) for the birds, leaves, buds, flowers, and bow. Add texture to the birds' bodies by topstitching (page 55). Try Grapes in Foil (page 67) for the berries. Optionally, add ink embellishments (page 43).

BASKET OF FRUIT AND FLOWERS

Symbolism

A basket is symbolically filled with blessings. Imagery of blessings fills this red (for love) basket tied in the original with a blue (for truth) bow. It holds symbolic fruit of the spirit, and in the flowers, the sweetness and beauty of a saved spirit. A bird and a butterfly, symbols for life of the soul, hover above the basket. Its pedestal is bound by yellow (the color of friendship). So here we have the colors of the Rebekahs, illustrating their motto, "Friendship, Love, and Truth." The Odd Fellow men had long used the cornucopia (often in links of red, yellow, blue) as their symbolic container for blessings. These symbols, in these colors, dance through Baltimore's Albums!

Vintage Inscription

But the fruit of the Spirit is love, joy, peace, long-suffering, gentleness, goodness, faith, meekness, temperance: against such there is no law.
—**Galatians 5:22–23**

Pattern Notes

One could, of course, make this basket of a solid piece of fabric, defining it with pedestal, brim, and handle.

Pattern Notes continue on page 115.

SCALLOPED EPERGNE OF FRUIT

Symbolism

The symbolism of this raised glass dish (in blue, for life of the soul) is surely that of the Basket block. Apple and bird stand alone, beside the pedestal—the bird, again, for life of the soul. An apple can symbolize many different things, among them love, youth, sin, and immortality.

Why Baltimore's Revival?

I really don't know as I am still planning from the Baltimore Album revival's previous "mini revival." Perhaps we realize that without the help and friendship of others our dreams will not become true without their love and assistance.
—**Sandra K. Rochon**

Pattern Notes

Epcrgnes, pedestaled ornamental glass serving dishes, were popular in the Album era. This simpler pattern comes from an 1846–1847 Album.

Pattern Notes continue on page 115.

BALTIMORE CLIPPER SHIP AND GARLAND

Symbolism

In Christian iconography a ship traditionally refers to the church; it can mean life's journey to salvation. Secularly it can simply mean life's journey. An anchor is a well-grounded hope, a last resort for firmness, tranquility, faithfulness. To Christians it symbolizes salvation. In many churches along the Baltic Sea, a sailing ship hangs above and to the left of the altar. In one church, on the frontmost sail, text in German reads, "Here I have found the soil where I can safely sink my anchor."

Vintage Inscription

One ship sails East, One ship sails West,
With the self-same wind that blows.
'Tis the set of the sails and not the gales
That determine the way she goes.

—**Old needlework inscription, verse by Ella Wheeler Wilcox, appears in Hamilton Sienkiewicz's birth sampler, cross-stitched by his mother.**

Pattern Notes

This center medallion is a joyous undertaking!

Pattern Notes continue on page 115.

QUILT AND PATTERN NOTES

VERDANT HEARTS, QUILT NOTES CONTINUED FROM page 15.
The quilt's center is inscribed: "To Mary Tozer from Baltimore's Daughters—Your loving friends, all. 2010. Verdant Hearts presented at TESAA's 15th, Williamsburg." Signed, "Elly Sienkiewicz scripset."

A brief history is inscribed beneath the inner border at the bottom of the quilt: "Mary's Verdant Hearts" (verdant: green, lush, growing, leafing out; hearts: symbolizing not only love, but also devotion).

"Dear Mary, You have linked so many hearts through Baltimore's Daughters, this grand show of Friendship Albums. So doing, you have won our eternal Affection. Bette suggested, stitched on, and set this quilt with those Dear Ones who have signed it. My privilege is to name this gift and inscribe it. Adding here my name and love. Thank you, Mary, from the bottom of our hearts! Quilted by Linda James in Bozeman, Montana." Signed "Elly Sienkiewicz scripset, January 2, 2010. Lewes, Delaware—Washington, D.C., USA."

While Bette designed and provided fabric and leadership, friends and group leaders like Kelly Kout, June Purpura, Tresa Jones, and those signed here brought this celebration to life!

PATTERN 1, PATTERN NOTES CONTINUED FROM page 86
Optionally, you can embroider (pages 55–60) serrated edges on the leaves using the blanket stitch, add top-stitched veins and moss rose, and add ink embellishments (page 43). Consider adding the banderole with Copperplate calligraphy (page 51) to the center of your block.

Note: This is my very favorite pattern to teach beginning to intermediate appliqué. The foliage teaches appliqué essentials: Points, Curves, and Inside Corners. Repetitiously, this pattern makes a quilter practice these essentials— learning with each repeat, improving even as she finishes the greenery. To then hop so quickly into the fancywork of dimensional appliqué buds breeds confidence and is a joy!

PATTERN 2, PATTERN NOTES CONTINUED FROM page 87
After making the Dual Fabric Rosebuds (page 78), slip each one into place under a calyx, pin-baste, and sew down the top edge of the bud. Remove template, pin bud in place, and appliqué calyx in place. Optionally, use the dashed line on the pattern for a bud template. Sew only the outside edges of each calyx, knotting off thread at the tip. Leave the ³⁄₁₆″ seam allowance inside of the calyxes cut, but not sewn. Sew the top of the bud down, then appliqué the inside calyx edges in place.

For the flowers use Freezer Paper Inside (page 29) or Needleturn (page 32), drawing the flower's turn-line and center onto the right side of the fabric. For the easiest center, fill its circle with colonial knots (page 57). For a one-of-a-kind dimensional flower, make Bette Augustine's Very Fancy Flowers (page 75) . Optionally, add ink embellishments (page 43).

PATTERN 7, PATTERN NOTES CONTINUED FROM page 92
In the antique, this simple rose was made from black wool, edged with a whip stitch. To echo that, 2 strands gold cotton floss could be used with a blanket stitch (page 59), the floral center could be filled with colonial knots (page 57). Prefer beads in the center and embroidered lyre strings? Try a stem stitch (page 56) in metallic gold, or even beads in a row (page 82). For the moss rose, hand embroider the blanket stitch in one strand of 50- to 60-weight sewing thread.

PATTERN 8, PATTERN NOTES CONTINUED FROM page 93
5. Cut 1 Template E for the rose.

6. Cut 1 Template F (½″ diameter) circle for the rose center.

Optionally, add 2 rows of colonial knots (page 57) in the rose center. Add rose moss (page 59 and ink embellishments (page 43).

PATTERN 10, PATTERN NOTES CONTINUED FROM page 95
2. Make 8 of the overleaf [C] from fusible-backed fabric (page 60). Instead of fusing the shape to the background, fold one in half lengthwise. Iron it to itself. Appliqué its fold

(from the dot down) over the flower and then appliqué its outside edge back up to the top of the leaf.

3. Draw shape [D] onto the appliqué. Fill it with colonial knots (page 57), then outline its shape with green outline stitch (page 56). Optionally, add ink embellishments (page 43).

PATTERN 12, PATTERN NOTES CONTINUED FROM page 97
Note: Enjoy close-in camerawork detailing this pattern's making on the DVD *Elly Sienkiewicz Teaches Advanced Baltimore Appliqué* (see Sources, page 126).

Then see page 80 for the Star Ruching technique for the blooms. Add rosebuds and small leaves using Separate Unit Appliqué (page31). Optionally, add ink embellishments (page 43) and rose moss (page 59).

PATTERN 13, PATTERN NOTES CONTINUED FROM page 98
Our thoroughly modern model by Anne Carter is ingenious: two flower shapes fused back-to-back for free-standing dimensionality. The buds, too, are a simple double-fused fan shape, cuffed and curled ice cream cone–like into wee trumpet flowerlike buds (her Double-Sided Flowers are on page 72).

Use Separate Unit Appliqué for the leaves, calyxes, and acorns (page 31). Or use Ultrasuede (page 60) for the acorns. Optionally, use colonial knots (page 37) for the acorn cap and add ink embellishments (page 43).

For a thoroughly innovative look and approach to baskets, try the Pin-Pad Transfer Method and diagonal weaving (pages 65–66).

PATTERN 14, PATTERN NOTES CONTINUED FROM page 99
When I've had the joy of teaching our peacock here, I've introduced Ultrasuede (page 60)—so easy for the eyes—and on the tail, silk ribbon, French wired ribbon, and beads. I've read: "For art to have meaning for the future, it must have the coin of its own time." And does not incorporating these fancy materials available to us give our work the coin of its own time?

PATTERN 15, PATTERN NOTES CONTINUED FROM page 100
Most Baltimore eagles are brown, some "Baltimore blue." Baltimoreans had colorfast indigo blue dye. Moreover, for these Judeo-Christians, blue symbolized truth, heaven, the divine. In Baltimore's Odd Fellows, the blue or royal degree was the third degree. The American flag is red (for love, valor, hardiness), white (for purity and innocence), and blue (for truth, vigilance, perseverance, and justice).

For the eye of the eagle, make a positioning template by making a paper pattern and cutting out the eye from the paper pattern. Use the open hole to trace the position of the eye onto the eagle appliqué fabric. To make the eye, fussy cut the eye from a print, or use white Ultrasuede (page 60), and ink the details with a Pigma pen (be sure to heat set using a tissue pressing cloth and a Synthetic setting on the iron—Ultrasuede acts like a sponge, and the ink can smear unless thoroughly dry). The eagle center medallion on the Williamsburg Album (page 16) has "eye feathers" edged in white Reverse Appliqué, a dramatic touch if there ever was one! Included at the 8″ block scale, this embellishment would be stem-stitched (page 56) in two strands of YLI white silk (or DMC cotton, a bit heavier) six-strand floss.

Flag lessons: Each white star represents a state on the blue square, called the canton. The 13 red stripes, for the original 13 colonies, are on the fly.

The flag stripes can be stitched many ways. Sandy Butler stitched hers by Cutaway (page 32), directly onto the print background. This augments the flow of open background—so typical of the classic Baltimore style. The following describes her technique.

1. Cut a rectangle of red 1″ larger all around than the pattern. Trace (over a lightbox) the stripes onto the red rectangle.

2. Pin the red rectangle right side up to the background, then stitch-baste (page 28) the top, middle, and last red stripe.

3. Cut the seam allowance 2″ at a time,* and needleturn appliqué. Begin with three close stitches where the drawn line begins. End the drawn line the same way, allowing a ⅛″ seam allowance. This underlap lies under the blue stars' field or under the pole at the left end. At the right end the excess gets shoved back (with a toothpick or embroidery scissors) into the stem at the end of each stripe.

*Note: You'll be cutting a channel between the red stripes, striving to cut evenly, giving both adjacent stripes the same seam allowance. Rather than draw the turn line, some folks baste carefully down the middle of each red stripe and cut, then turn under until the basting stitches stop the turn. They call this otherwise unmarked Cutaway "Channel Appliqué."

The shield is also a great place to try Kathy Dunigan's straight-cut cotton Skinny-Skinny Stems (page 63). Remember, please, in appliqué, your way is the best way!

The garland includes edge-stitched serrate leaves using a series of straight stitches (page 60) and single-thread legged French knots (page 57). Other flower centers include clustered colonial knots (page 57), bead embroidery (page 82), and beads-in-a-row (page 82). Optionally, add ink embellishments (page 43).

Flagpole Finial

Topping off the flagpole with a stencil-shaded Ultrasuede finial provides a glorious touch on this block. Follow these steps:

1. Create a stencil from a 1½" × 2" square of freezer paper as follows: Trace half of the pattern on freezer paper, fold it in half, and cut double with the shiny side of the freezer paper facing in. The drawn line stays on the cut template. Note that the base of the finial must fit the width of the pole—it is easier to adjust the finial base than to re-appliqué the pole!

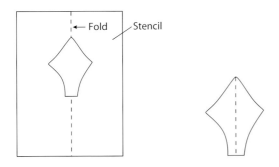

2. Iron the window template onto the right side of a 2" × 2½" rectangle of Ultrasuede fabric, and stabilize the back of the finial fabric with masking tape.

3. The window template is now your artist's palette. Scribble a dime-sized dot each of light shade (yellow ochre), medium shade (burnt sienna), and dark shade (burnt umber) around the perimeter of the finial shape. I like to use Sakura Specialist Oil Pastels for this process.

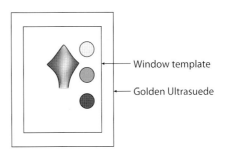

4. Pull a swatch of quilt-weight cotton taut over your forefinger. Outline the whole finial with the light shade, pushing the oil pastel over the edge of the window template onto the fabric, working the color into the finial. Then push the medium shade slightly less far.

5. At this stage, you can create an optional linear detail. Iron two 1" × 2" rectangles of freezer paper across the stenciled finial spaced horizontally about ⅛" apart at the widest part of the finial shape. (Be sure to use a tissue press cloth.) Push the dark shade over the horizontal edges working the color less than ⅛" into the finial.

6. Darkening the very outer edge is tricky at this small scale. Cut the window template back ¼" or so to create an oval. Push the oil pastel finger brush down outside the finial outline, then inward to darken just the outer edge.

7. Using the cut-out freezer-paper finial image as a template, cut out the Ultrasuede finial so that no unstenciled fabric shows beyond the stencil shading. Heat-set with a tissue press cloth. Gluestick baste the finial in place over the ⅛″ flagpole underlap and tack stitch (page 29) using matching or neutral thread, and listen for the happy buzz of admiration!

Three-Dimensional Tassels

Tassels are an elegant embellishment for an appliquéd flag. Follow this procedure to make one. On an antique quilt, the stem-stitched tassel cord showed, embroidered on the background cloth, which served as the flag's foundation. This tells us something about the sequence in which the block was made … perhaps!

1. Make a ¾″ × 2″ winding bobbin out of a file folder. Cut it double, if desired, for strength. It is cut long for ease of handling. Notch both long sides to create the ¼″ wrap bridge.

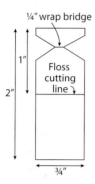

2. Choose a 6-strand floss to wind; cotton and wool both work.

3. Use repositionable tape to attach the floss's start to the file folder.

4. Wrap until you sense that you are done. The tendency is to wrap too much: Remember the tassel will be twice the front thickness. Tape down the tail when done winding.

5. Slip an 8″-long strand of 3-ply floss under the top loops, and tie off tightly behind the tassel. Cut off the tails of the knot.

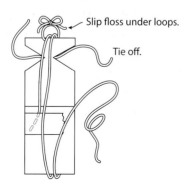

6. Tape the floss to the file folder, front and back above the floss cutting line.

7. Cut the front and back floss at the floss cutting line. Clip the tape and remove the card.

8. Tie off the waist, knotting behind the tassel, and cutting off the tails. The tassel measures ⅞″ long; trim to taste.

9. Stem stitch (page 56) the tassel cord, hidden by the flag, or let the stem stitching show.

10. Attach the tassel with matching YLI 100-weight silk thread (see Sources, page 126). Couch (page 55) the tassel to within ⅛″ of the bottom to allow a little play.

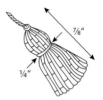

PATTERN 17, PATTERN NOTES CONTINUED FROM page 102

To minimally mark the leaves, put an arrow at the top tip, a dot at bottom center, and connect them with a line, like this: ◄————————•. Pin-place (page 85) before stitching. Connect the leaves to main stems, chain-stitching (page 58) a double row with 2 strands of floss. Don't those grapes invite experimentation with needlework perfection? (See Perfect Circles and Grapes in Foil, page 67.) For each grape, simply mark a dot where its center should be on the background and mark a center dot on the grape/circle template. Try some inkwork (page 43)—inking the tendrils invites thickening the downstroke for a historic look.

PATTERN 18, PATTERN NOTES CONTINUED FROM page 103

This pattern can really be sped up: Begin with Stems Made in-Hand (page 62), ¼″ inside the top solid rose line on both stems. Pin, then stitch-baste them in place using big stitches. By the time you've placed the roses there is so little stem left to sew!

Split leaves (page 66): Machine sew (¼″ seam) 2 different print strips, each 1½″ wide, together. Iron the seams to one side. Cut the sandwiched seam down to ⅛″ wide. Turn each leaf's ¼″ seam over freezer paper with a gluestick (page 30). Ruche the roses (page 80). Adjust the ruched strip's length to cover the dotted line drawn on the background. The rose centers can be yo-yos (page 73), fringes (page 74), colonial knots (page 57), or a Rolled Rose center (page 75) on top of a ruched outer row. Or, beads in a row (page 82) can surround a simple appliquéd center. Add serrated leaf edges using a blanket stitch (page 59) and add topstitching (page 55) to define the leaf veins. Optionally, add ink embellishments (page 43).

PATTERN 20, PATTERN NOTES CONTINUED FROM page 105

I learned last year that there was a Women's Division of the Design School of the Maryland Institute. Principles of art were being studied by women in Baltimore, and it shows! The balanced asymmetry of this pattern is so elegant and precarious that I would go out of my way to ensure that the dove and particularly the anchor, then the bow, are placed carefully. The curved part of the anchor is perpendicular to the vertical center of the block, and its upright bar is parallel to the vertical centerline of the block. One of the best renditions of the chain was embroidered in large, loose chain stitch (page 58) with heavy size 5 perle cotton!

Use Cutaway Appliqué (page 32) for the wreath, widening the ends to form a calyx. Appliqué them in place after the rosebuds are inserted. Use Separate Unit Appliqué (page 31) for the leaves, calyxes and rosebuds, dove, anchor, and bow. Use Fusible Appliqué (page 60) to make the bird's eye.

PATTERN 21, PATTERN NOTES CONTINUED FROM page 106

For the shapes, use Separate Unit Appliqué (page 31) and Skinny-Skinny Stems (page 63).

Embroider the pussy willow stems with 2 rows of chain stitch (page 58), sewn with 2 strands of 6-strand cotton floss; and the finer stems adjoining the leaves with 1 row of chain stitch, sewn with a single strand of floss. Add a colonial knot (page 57) at the end of each pussy willow.

For the flowers, embroider the divisions of the petals with chain stitch and 2 rows of colonial knots sewn with 3 strands of floss to surround the flower appliqué fabric left bare at the flower's center. Leave a bit of petal appliqué fabric uncovered at its center. Add rose moss (page 59) as the final details.

PATTERN 23, PATTERN NOTES CONTINUED FROM page 108

Or make it a slat basket with vertical ribbon slats. On the other hand, this scoop-sided basket is a classic! And you can do it. It would be easiest with Trifold Stems made super-skinny (page 62). These Skinny-Skinny Stems are perfect for

the foliage stems also. Use Separate Unit Appliqué (page 31) for the shapes, and try Grapes in Foil (page 68) for the berries. Stem stitching and French knots (page 56) add detail to the butterfly, and colonial knots (page 57) finish the centers of the roses. Use stem stitches (page 56) for the tiniest leaf stems. Try the painting techniques on pages 43–47 to add shading to the fruit, birds, and butterfly.

PATTERN 24, PATTERN NOTES CONTINUED FROM page 109

My sense is that the more ornate epergnes followed. Dr. Dunton (author of *Old Quilts*) notes, "The upper bunch of grapes is blue, the lower red. The three strawberries to the right are red, their seeds indicated with white stitching." Because we are all familiar with realistic paintings of fruit, this is an excellent block on which to practice using art material (pages 41–82). Footnote to history: *Epergne* is in Webster's, but rare. Its use here honors my English grandmother, Nana, whose set of plain glass epergnes I inherited and split with my niece Erica, who also loves them.

The appliqué in this block is straightforward; use Separate Unit Appliqué (page31) for the shapes. Try Perfect Grapes (page 67) for the berries, and use the same method described for Split Leaves (page 66) for the fruit. Stems can be applied using Skinny-Skinny Stems (page 63). A satin stitch (page 58) completes the bird's beak, and the eye can be made using Fusible Appliqué (page 60). This is another excellent block for stencil shading (pages 48–49).

PATTERN 25, PATTERN NOTES CONTINUED FROM page 110

Start with the masts, then the sails (for oil pastel stencil shading of the sails or acrylic color wash, see pages 43–49), the boat, the sea, and the garland. Want to know more about ship nomenclature and colorful history? See www.eraoftheclipperships.com!

Use couching (page 55) for the rigging, stem stitching with colonial knots for the flower tendrils, lazy daisy stitches (page 34, covered in outside points earlier) for ferns, and rose mosss (page 59) to give texture to the buds. For the garland, try stencil-shaded roses (page 48), shell ruching (page 79), or Showy Ruched Ribbon Roses (page 81) with colonial knots (page 57) to finish the rose centers.

Needleartists are those volunteers who contributed their stitchery on a non-professional basis. The professional setter and quilters are so appreciated as well. Each of 245 volunteers (gentlewomen and one gentleman) contributed considerable time and talent to the Baltimore's Daughters quilts pictured herein. Some wrote a brief biography for the historic record and offered thoughts on why, in these postmodern times, Baltimore-style quilts (and their revivalist daughters) have been so well loved for so long. Devoted professional quiltmakers set the quilts, although Marla Landt, Tresa Jones, and Marjorie Lydecker each set the group quilt they led. Skilled professionals quilted all but Marjorie Lydecker's quilt, as noted in the Gallery notes. At Elly's behest, this cyberspace, friendship-bound, world-wide community helped make these contemporary revivalist Baltimore Album Quilts. That it was accomplished and has resulted in a major exhibition and this book says magnificently good things about quilters!

The old Album style was set by women (in an age where humility and service were anticipated and approved) living through social revolution (exciting, unnerving) in a new nation on the move. They picked up their needles and stitched in community. We moderns, working in community, also want to feel a part of history, to gift history with what we have learned, gift her with the comforting touch of another's warmth and wisdom, gift her with that beauty that is always from God. Baltimore's old Album Quilts are fascinating ladies. Ladies who, after three decades of scholars' scrutiny and quiltmakers'

faithful replications and vivacious innovations, remain world-class beauties, but still … women of mystery. We know so much about the quiltmakers of antebellum Baltimore City, Maryland, and yet so little. We moderns who helped make these revivalist quilts want to leave a more legible "footprint" for the future, a few trail markers to set history off on the right path. Humbly, should

Western civilization itself survive, I believe these quilts will again be brought to the sun's light, generations from now. We, Baltimore's children, aspire thereby to give comfort and joy to hearts yet unborn. Brief biographies follow for the stitchers of *Happiness Is in the Journey*, patterned herein. For thee, Dear Reader, and for history, these modest trail markers follow.

HAPPINESS IS IN THE JOURNEY
(QUILT ON **PAGE 12**)

A1	B1	C1	D1	E1	F1
A2	B2	C2	D2	E2	F2
A3	B3			E3	F3
A4	B4	Medallion		E4	F4
A5	B5	C5	D5	E5	F5
A6	B6	C6	D6	E6	F6

Donna Anderson

Block E3   Donna has always been interested in Baltimore Album Quilts. When she took a Baltimore Album class with Marjorie Lydecker she became a hand appliqué, piecing, and quilting devotee because of Marge's enthusiasm and dedication to the craft. She is honored to be part of this generation of Baltimore quilts and hopes they will be honored in future generations as the originals are today. Donna is from Plymouth, MA.

Bette F. Augustine

Blocks A1, F5   A former legal secretary and librarian, Bette is the beloved administrator for the annual Elly Sienkiewicz Appliqué Academy. Married 42 years, she has two amazing children and two beautiful granddaughters. Bette lives in Hemet, CA.

Sandy Butler

Block D2   Sandy's love of quilting came from her mother, who is still appliquéing Mary Simon blocks at the age of 86. Sandy started with embroidery and progressed to hand piecing when her three daughters left home. However, when she discovered appliqué, she was hooked and now finds it the most satisfying and challenging. Sandy lives in Gibsonton, FL.

Anne Carter

Block A4   Anne is a devoted wife, a mother of two wonderful daughters, a fraternal twin, and a certified public accountant. Her inspiration to become a quilter was instantaneous when she attended the Vermont Quilt Show some years ago. She began as a self-taught quilter and has since attended one of Elly's excellent classes as well as classes with other talented teachers. Anne lives in Rochester, NH.

Connie Chapman

Blocks B6, E6   Connie is a wife, a mother, and very new to appliqué. She loves the process and the serenity that descends on her as she takes little stitch after little stitch. Connie lives in St. Michael, MN.

Jennifer C. Chapman

Block A3   Jennifer loves travel and adventure. She has been to the Amazon, Egypt, Jordan, Tanzania, and more. Each Baltimore-style block is an adventure, with no two the same. To make a quilt where each block was alike would bore her to tears! Jennifer lives in Hingham, MA.

Patricia Clayton
Block A5   Patricia's mother instilled in her a love of needlework; appliqué was her first love. She took a class with Elly and has been on a Baltimore Album journey ever since. Patricia is from Westborough, MA.

Carol Henn Cooper
Block B5   Carol is a needleartist from Strafford, NH.

Elaine Dwyer
Block D1   Elaine is a needleartist from Centerville, MA.

Debbie Eaton
Block B3   Debbie discovered Baltimore Album Quilts in 1983 when she came upon Elly's book *Spoken Without a Word,* and her life would never be the same. She's not sure which she enjoys most: the making of a quilt or sharing her enthusiasm through teaching others about the Album Quilts. Debbie lives in Groton, MA.

Marjorie J. Farquharson
Block B1   As an elementary school librarian, Marjorie was originally attracted to Baltimore Album Quilts not only for their beauty but for the stories behind the designs. When she works on the appliqué for an Album Quilt, she savors the journey as much as the finished quilt. Marjorie is from Needham, MA.

Jan Fish
Block C1   Jan is a needleartist from Weymouth, MA.

Deborah Fournier-Johnstone
Block E2   Deborah is a needleartist from Dover, NH.

Suzanne Fox
Block A6   Suzanne is a wife, mother, nurse, and gardener. When Suzanne was a child, her mother taught her needle-arts. In the late 1970s, she started quilting by taking classes. Twenty years ago a friend challenged her to try appliqué, and Suzanne's first appliqué quilt was a miniature Album Quilt. She has worked on various styles since then. Suzanne lives in Hanover, MA.

Mary Furber
Block B2   Mary is a native of New Milford, CT, and currently resides in Portsmouth, NH. She has been working with fabric since she was a child and has experience in quilting, quilt pattern design, embroidery, penny rugs, and rug hooking. After working as a computer programmer for many years, she now owns Little Lamb Quilt Shop in Barrington, NH.

Sue Hart
Block D6   Sue has been fortunate to learn from Elly and truly appreciates the history of Baltimore Album Quilts. She treasures the many new friendships she's made through the connections of Baltimore classes and lectures. Sue is from Norwell, MA.

Minnie Jackson
Block C5   Minnie started quilting in 2001, and has made about 100 quilts. She works full-time as a 911 operator, and spent three years and three months hand-piecing her *Dear Jane* quilt, which she will quilt in the near future. Appliqué is her first love and brings her many hours of joy and peace, whether she has a needle in hand or is admiring the works of others. Her wish is that she will have passed on some of this love to her children and grandchildren so that they may keep the art of quilting alive. Minnie lives in Dunedin, FL.

Jean F. Kearney
Block F6   A quiltmaker since the 1970s, Jean has a love for quilts and the process. This connection to the past has led her to achieve certification as a quilt instructor; to participate as a member of AQSG, AQS, NEQM, the Cocheco Quilt Guild, and the DLM Quilt Group of NH; and to volunteer for the NEQM and the NHQDP. Jean believes the Baltimore Album Quilts reflect the preservation of legacy with a permanent gift of research, documentation, and re-created patterns for all ages. Jean is from Durham, NH.

Maryann McFee
Dogtooth Border   Maryann own Mare's Bears Quilt Shop in Lewes, DE. She was fortunate to meet Elly about 10 years ago. Elly has inspired Maryann and her shop over the years. Her wonderful husband, Doug, has encouraged her endeavor over the past 30 years. They have four daughters, one son, five grandchildren, and two great-grandchildren. Maryann's love for quilting started in the 1980s and has never stopped. Maryann lives in Lewes, DE.

Connie Mooers
Block C2   Connie is a needleartist from South Dennis, MA.

June Moore
Blocks E5, F1   June often reflects on the Baltimore Album Quilts made by our long-ago sisters, who found time to stitch something so wonderful—little did they know that these quilts would survive and be with us today. June is from Isanti, MN.

Karen Moraal
Block A2   Over the years, Karen's love of quilting has turned into a passion. It has been a sanctuary for her as a single mother with two boys. In a very hectic and demanding life, appliqué and quilting help center her soul and express who she is. Karen is from Westborough, MA.

Marlyn Morey
Block F4   Upon high school graduation, Marlyn was torn between her love for sewing and fabric and her love for mathematics. She attended the Fashion Institute of Technology for a brief time and then spent her career in accounting. Marlyn has been quilting since 1996 and loves quilt history and traditional quilt patterns. Appliqué has become addictive for her! Marlyn lives in Spring Hill, FL.

Karen Pessia
Block F2   Karen has been a quilter for more than 25 years; Baltimore Albums came into her life 6 years ago. The classes she has taken to learn appliqué and to learn about these beautiful Album Quilts have brought many wonderful people, new friendships, experiences, and teaching into her world. Karen lives in Medford, MA.

Cate Rosendale
Block E4   Cate is a needleartist and beloved appliqué teacher from San Antonio, FL.

Kathy Spielman
Block E1   Kathy was introduced to Baltimore Album Quilts when Elly Sienkiewicz taught a class for the Cocheco Quilt Guild. She loves to crazy quilt and embellish her quilts, and Elly's flowers and techniques provided new ideas for her projects. She enjoyed working on her block and the border for *Happiness Is in the Journey,* incorporating these new techniques. Kathy is from Durham, NH.

Diane DeVido Tetreault

Block B4   Diane has been quilting for more than 25 years. Elly's quilts have always inspired and challenged her. She loved working on her block—it pushed her beyond her normal limits and was incredibly rewarding. Diane is from Wellesley, MA.

Carrie Thompson

Block C6   Carrie comes from a family of quilters and has always been fascinated by quilt patterns and designs. Every block she has made has a story about what was happening in her life at the time and where she was traveling while she worked on it. Carrie is fascinated by the women who made the original Album Quilts and wonders about the stories behind their blocks. Carrie is from Wellesley, MA.

Mary K. Tozer

Blocks C3/C4, D3/D4 (center medallion)   Mary was bitten by the quilting bug in 1990 and became enamored with appliqué and the Baltimore Album Quilts around 2000. Her career has changed a number of times from being a student, which led to a handful of years as a geologist, to now working for a major agricultural company. The two constant obsessions in her life, however, are her family and all things connected to quilting. Mary lives in Rogers, MN.

Janice D. Vaine

Block F3   At the age of five, Jan's mother instilled in her a love for all things needle and thread. Now in midlife, her love has blossomed into a small pattern-design company. It has also afforded Jan the opportunity to teach and share miniature piecing, needleturn appliqué, and embroidery. Jan says, "There is heartfelt joy in watching others fall in love with the gentle rhythm of needle and thread passing through fabric. Our needleart journeys are truly balm for the soul." Janice lives in Jacksonville, FL.

Bobbie M. Wendell

Block D5   After retirement Bobbie took an appliqué course with Deb Eaton of Groton, MA, where she fell in love with this needleart. During most of her life she has loved sewing—the process of putting fabrics together into a beautiful picture became a method of artistic expression. For Bobbie, there is no way to measure the countless hours of creative joy that appliqué has provided. Bobbie lives in Dummerston, VT.

DEAR FRIENDS REMEMBERED (QUILT ON page 16)

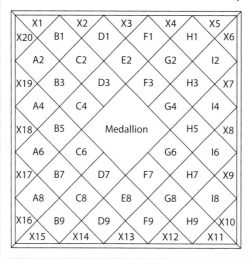

A2	Patricia Sherer Cotter	Houston, TX
A4	Cathy L. Graves	Knoxville, TN
A6	Janice D. Vaine	Jacksonville, FL
A8	Jeni Buechel	South Park, PA
B1	JoAnn Cridge	Pittsburgh, PA
B3	Ellen T. Armstrong	Richmond, VA
B5	Mara K. Warwick	Ankara, Turkey
B7	Kathleen L. Osgood	Huntington Beach, CA
B9	Nadine E. Thompson	Springfield, MO
C2	Ann O'Rafferty	Dublin, Ireland
C4	Nancy Kerns	Skillman, NJ
C6	Beverly J. Gamble	Westfield, MA
C8	Teri Levin	Charleston, SC
D1	Patricia A. Clayton	Westborough, MA
D3	Christine Maxwell Bonney	Queensland, Australia
Medallion	Emily S. Martin	Woodbridge, VA
D7	JoAnn S. Hudgins	Garland, TX
D9	Mary K. Tozer	Rogers, MN
E2	Dr. Suzan Aufiero	Cogan Station, PA
E8	Connie Chapman	St. Michael, MN
F1	Laura P. Deschamps	Callander, Ontario, Canada
F3	Katherine Scott Hudgins Dunigan	Oakville, Ontario, Canada
F7	Georgann Spikes Wrinkle	Houston, TX
F9	Susan L. Powell	Madbury, NH
G2	Karen Moraal	Westborough, MA
G4	Jeanne A. Sullivan	Annapolis, MD
G6	Kaye Tennyson-Smith	Chestertown, NY
G8	Mary K. Tozer	Rogers, MN
H1	Susan Day	Providence, RI
H3	Patti Ives	Spring Creek, NV
H5	Linda Goodejohn	Sammamish, WA
H7	Diane Coleman Wilson	Swansea, IL
H9	Melissa S. Mattz	Riverside, CA
I2	Katherine Tennyson	Chestertown, NY
I4	Elizabeth Bonsack Strader-Sweeney	Blackburg, VA
I6	Joanne Parks	Northbrook, IL
I8	Marjorie A. Nelson	Frankfort, MI
X1	Sheva Farkas	Silver Spring, MD
X2	Robin J. Buscemi	Wilmette, IL
X3	Sheva Farkas	Silver Spring, MD
X4	Katherine Sperry McMullen	O'Fallon, IL
X5	Robin J. Buscemi	Wilmette, IL
X6	Kari Lippert	Hanover, MD
X7	Patricia Konze	O'Fallon, IL
X8	Lynne Huneault	Burlington, Ontario, Canada
X9	Lynne Huneault	Burlington, Ontario, Canada
X10	Yvonne Brady	Dublin, Ireland
X11	Katherine Sperry McMullen	O'Fallon, IL
X12	Sheva Farkas	Silver Spring, MD
X13	Kari Lippert	Hanover, MD
X14	Katherine Sperry McMullen	O'Fallon, IL
X15	Robin Buscemi	Wilmette, IL
X16	Kari Lippert	Hanover, MD
X17	Patricia Konze	O'Fallon, IL
X18	Angela Cotter	Dublin, Ireland
X19	Lynne Huneault	Burlington, Ontario, Canada
X20	Patricia Konze	O'Fallon, IL

LET US BE FRIENDS (QUILT ON page 17)

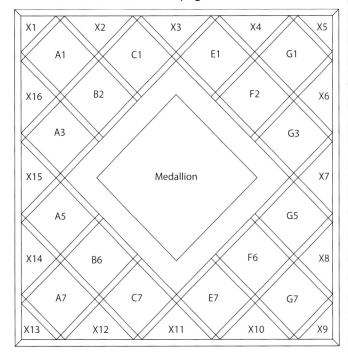

A1			

(Diagram grid labels:)

X1 X2 X3 X4 X5
A1 C1 E1 G1
X16 B2 F2 X6
A3 G3
X15 Medallion X7
A5 G5
X14 B6 F6 X8
A7 C7 E7 G7
X13 X12 X11 X10 X9

A1	Pamela Harris	Watsonville, CA
A3	Kathleen Mary Gray	Glen Ellen, CA
A5	Diana Tatro	Yuba City, CA
A7	Mary Ann Bloom	Turlock, CA
B2	Myra K. Forbyn	Placerville, CA
B6	Nellie Hungerford	Sunnyvale, CA
C1	Marlene Chapple	Valley Springs, CA
Medallion	Marsha J. Smith	Fair Oaks, CA
	Mary K. Tozer	Rogers, MN
C7	Sharon Lampton	Napa, CA
E1	Kathleen H. Gordon	Yuba City, CA
E7	Bonnie Cantoni	Wallace, CA
F2	Sheila Patterson Bayley	Fair Oaks, CA
F6	Lynne I. Storm	Valley Springs, CA
G1	Dana Lahargoue	Folsom, CA
G3	Marsha J. Smith	Fair Oaks, CA
G5	Barbara Phillips-Barrett	Yountville, CA
G7	Robin Asby	Yuba City, CA
X1	Don Elgia Hancock	Fremont, CA
X2	Cora Velasco	San Jose, CA
X3	Don Elgia Hancock	Fremont, CA
X4	Don Elgia Hancock	Fremont, CA
X5	Don Elgia Hancock	Fremont, CA
X6	Virginia McCurdy	Fremont, CA
X7	Marina Rosario	Lebanon, OR
X8	Virginia McCurdy	Fremont, CA
X9	June Marie Purpura	Novato, CA
X10	Cora Velasco	San Jose, CA
X11	Tonie Brown	Novato, CA
X12	Robin Asby	Yuba City, CA
X13	June Marie Purpura	Novato, CA
X14	Don Elgia Hancock	Fremont, CA
X15	Marina Rosario	Lebanon, OR
X16	Tonie Brown	Novato, CA

AFFECTION'S TRIBUTE (QUILT ON page 18)

(Diagram grid labels:)

A1 B1 C1 D1 E1 F1
A2 B2 C2 D2 E2 F2
A3 B3 E3 F3
A4 B4 Medallion E4 F4
A5 B5 C5 D5 E5 F5
A6 B6 C6 D6 E6 F6

A1	Denise Poslusny	Lewes, DE
A2	JoAnne Yarnell	West Chester, PA
A3	Rosanne Menacker	Hockessin, DE
A4	Louise C. Morrow	Allentown, PA
A5	Shirley V. Collins	Rehoboth Beach, DE
A6	Deborah Vernon Haley	Hockessin, DE
B1	Donna Howard	Watertown, SD
B2	Tresa Jones	Seneca, KS
B3	Patricia A. Christ	Kempton, PA
B4	JoAnne Yarnall	West Chester, PA
B5	Tina Cole	Annapolis, MD
B6	Vonna M. Hotchkin	Salisbury, MD
C1	Teri Weed	Wynnewood, PA
C2	Teri Weed	Wynnewood, PA
Medallion	Nancy Kerns	Skillman, NJ
C5	Robyn L. MacKay	Pittsgrove, NJ
C6	Dorothy W. Murdoch	West Chester, PA
D1	Robyn L. MacKay	Pittsgrove, NJ
D2	Joyce Barone	Milford, DE
D5	Mary A. Showalter	Felton, DE
D6	Katherine Sydnor	Kinsdale, VA
E1	Bette Adams Stubbs	Moneta, VA
E2	Kelly Kout	Bowie, MD
E3	Betty Akana	Milford, DE
E4	Kelly Kout	Bowie, MD
E5	Kathy Delaney	Overland Park, KS
E6	Ruby C. Jones	Dagsboro, DE
F1	Fran Lopes	Easton, MD
F2	Kathy Delaney	Overland Park, KS
F3	Lynn Smith	Chesapeake, VA
F4	Maryann McFee	Lewes, DE
F5	Jo Ann Martin	Edgewater, MD
F6	Melissa Jean Papajohn	Harper's Ferry, WV
Outer Borders	Tresa Jones	Seneca, KS

THINK OF ME, DEAR ONE (QUILT ON page 19)

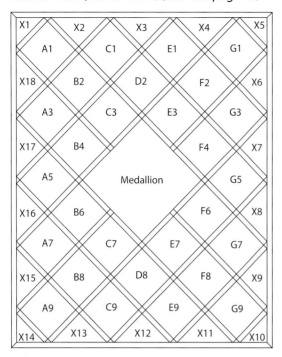

X1	X2	X3	X4	X5
A1	C1	E1	G1	
X18	B2	D2	F2	X6
A3	C3	E3	G3	
X17	B4	F4	X7	
A5	Medallion	G5		
X16	B6	F6	X8	
A7	C7	E7	G7	
X15	B8	D8	F8	X9
A9	C9	E9	G9	
X14	X13	X12	X11	X10

A1	Dawn Wakelam Hunt	Canmore, Alberta, Canada
A3	Barbara Gerow Ruault	Cochrane, Alberta, Canada
A5	Betty Bailey	Cochrane, Alberta, Canada
A7	Fauntie P. Phillips	Yorkton, Saskatchewan, Canada
A9	Fauntie P. Phillips	Yorkton, Saskatchewan, Canada
B2	Bette Adams Stubbs	Moneta, VA
B4	Kari Lippert	Hanover, MD
B6	Stella M. Blunt	West Newbury, MA
B8	Marcie Lane	Ajax, Ontario, Canada
C1	Debra Anger	Scarborough, Ontario, Canada
C3	Lynne Huneault	Burlington, Ontario, Canada
Medallion	Katherine Scott Hudgins Dunigan	Oakville, Ontario, Canada
C7	Mara K. Warwick	Ankara, Turkey
C9	Marie E. Collins	Calgary, Alberta, Canada
D2	Karen Julian	Smiths Falls, Ontario, Canada
D8	JoAnn S. Hudgins	Garland, TX
E1	Eileen G. Cole	Cochrane, Alberta, Canada
E3	Anne Barney	Bradford, MA
E7	Patricia Hansen	Killeen, TX
E9	Ruth Thrush	Cochrane, Alberta, Canada
F2	Monica Bishop	Three Hills, Alberta, Canada
F4	Annette E. Johnston	Red Deer, Alberta, Canada
F6	Mary Cargill	New York, NY
F8	JoAnn S. Hudgins	Garland, TX
G1	Mary Lou Zuck	Cochrane, Alberta, Canada
G3	Betty Bailey	Cochrane, Alberta, Canada
G5	Marcie Lane	Ajax, Ontario, Canada
G7	Lynne Huneault	Burlington, Ontario, Canada
G9	Yvonne Miller	Cochrane, Alberta, Canada
X1	Katherine Scott Hudgins Dunigan	Oakville, Ontario, Canada
X2	Karen Julian	Smiths Falls, Ontario, Canada
X3	Mary Lou Zuck	Cochrane, Alberta, Canada
X4	Betty Bailey	Cochrane, Alberta, Canada
X5	Katherine Scott Hudgins Dunigan	Oakville, Ontario, Canada
X6	Mara Warwick	Ankara, Turkey
X7	Annette E. Johnston	Red Deer, Alberta, Canada
X8	Debra Anger	Scarborough, Ontario, Canada
X9	Mary Cargill	New York, NY
X10	Katherine Scott Hudgins Dunigan	Oakville, Ontario, Canada
X11	Sandra Rochon	Calgary, Alberta, Canada
X12	Stella M. Blunt	West Newbury, MA
X13	Anne Barney	Bradford, MA
X14	Katherine Scott Hudgins Dunigan	Oakville, Ontario, Canada
X15	Patricia Hansen	Killeen, TX
X16	Bette Adams Stubbs	Moneta, VA
X17	Eileen G. Cole	Cochrane, Alberta, Canada
X18	Dawn Wakelam Hunt	Canmore, Alberta, Canada
Border	Katherine Scott Hudgins Dunigan	Oakville, Ontario, Canada

HAPPY HOURS, SWEETLY SPENT (QUILT ON page 20)

A1	B1	C1	D1	E1	F1
A2	B2	C2	D2	E2	F2
A3	B3			E3	F3
A4	B4	Medallion		E4	F4
A5	B5	C5	D5	E5	F5
A6	B6	C6	D6	E6	F6

A1	Karin Kratzer Crawford	Arcadia, CA
A2	Marla Duenwald Landt	Anchorage, AK
A3	Susan Marie Bryan	Colorado Springs, CO
A4	Connie M. Tabor	Blackfoot, ID
A5	Ruth Timothy	Brigham City, UT
A6	Pattie Webb	Anchorage, AK
B1	Pam Ventgen	Anchorage, AK
B2	Carolyn Goff Kimble	Moss Point, MS
B3	Ruth Timothy	Brigham City, UT
B4	Pam Ventgen	Anchorage, AK
B5	Dorothy Arab	Seattle, WA
B6	Carolyn Goff Kimble	Moss Point, MS
C1	Elaine Gummersheimer	Steelville, MO
C2	Pat Anderson	Littleton, CO
Medallion	Marla Duenwald Landt	Anchorage, AK
C5	Jana Vosika	Idaho Falls, ID
C6	Pam Ventgen	Anchorage, AK
D1	Bobbie Shields	Grand Forks, ND
D2	Linda K. James	Bozeman, MT
D5	Jana Vosika	Idaho Falls, ID
D6	Sue Ferry	Salt Lake City, UT
E1	Sandra Wyngaard	Mountain Home, ID
E2	Jana Vosika	Idaho Falls, ID
E3	Elaine Gummersheimer	Steelville, MO
E4	Linda K. James	Bozeman, MT
E5	Cindy Thiel	Missoula, MT
E6	Pat Anderson	Littleton, CO
F1	Dorothy Arab	Seattle, WA
F2	Pattie Webb	Anchorage, AK
F3	Bobbie Shields	Grand Forks, ND
F4	Carolyn Goff Kimble	Moss Point, MS
F5	Cheryl Bowers	Coolin, ID
F6	Sandra J. Wyngaard	Mountain Home, ID

SWEET REMEMBRANCE (QUILT ON page 21)

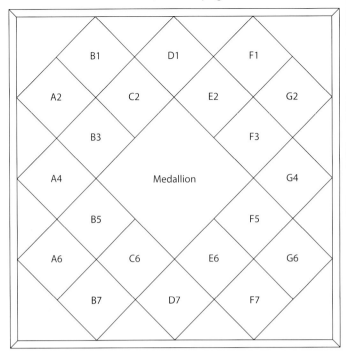

A2	Pauline J. Mallory	Largo, FL
A4	Susan E. Lorenz	Largo, FL
A6	Laurie Flowers	Jacksonville, FL
B1	Jan Compagnon	Jacksonville, FL
B3	Martha Choate Nash	Charlotte, NC
B5	Ronda Woods	Orange Park, FL
B7	Cathy Starman	Seminole, FL
C2	Rebecca Madasz	Palm Harbor, FL
Medallion	Lynda Feldman Weingart	Largo, FL
	Marguerite Connolly	Broomfield, CO
C6	Dorothy M. Oliva	St. Petersburg, FL
D1	Louise S. Rothman	Gainesville, FL
D7	Susan E. Lorenz	Largo, FL
E2	Carol Clarke	Seminole, FL
E6	Marva Gurley	Largo, FL
F1	Lori Lewis	Clearwater, FL
F3	Ellen Lemaux	Charlotte, NC
F5	Genia Holland	Anderson, SC
F7	Melanie Page Jensen	Gainesville, FL
G2	Elizabeth S. Mann	Largo, FL
G4	Gayle Craddock Larsen	Middleburg, FL
G6	Claudette Prevot	Jacksonville, FL

THROUGH TUFTS OF BROIDERED FLOWERS
(QUILT ON page 15)

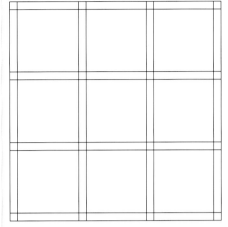

Blocks made by Susan Kurth and inked by Elly Sienkiewicz

Though Susan Kurth lives in Oklahoma and I in our nation's capital, we met through decades of classes together. *Through Tufts of Broidered Flowers* began by my asking Susan to make a teaching model using my new fabric line. She continued making blocks of her choice, having suggested that we make a quilt together. When I confessed myself unable to even begin a block, Susan said, "That's okay, you can do the inscriptions and inking, design the setting, and have it quilted."

To Susan's joyous use of prints and intensive embroidered embellishment, I added an antique reproduction set/border fabric that looked wondrously like the Russian culture from whence I, though born a Scots-Irish Hamilton, had come. Susan, long a student of literature, provided the snatches of poetry (from "The Abdication of Noman," by Richard Henry Stoddard) inscribed on our quilt, and its well-suited name. This first-born Daughter of Baltimore was started in Jackson Hole, Wyoming, in 2005, and the quilting was finished in 2009.

OUR SUMMER JOURNEY (QUILT ON page 14)

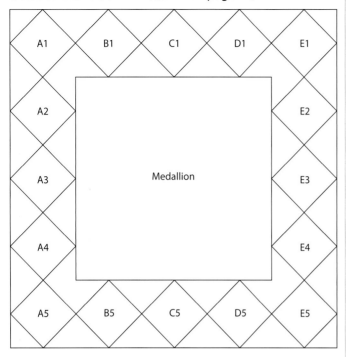

FAITH, HOPE, AND LOVE (QUILT ON page 22)

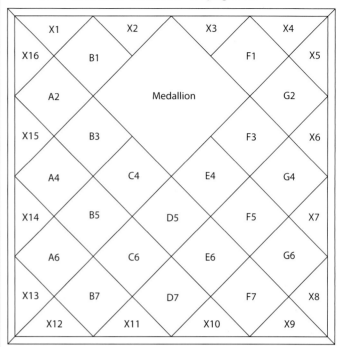

A1	Betsy Jackson	*Norwell, MA*
A2	Lee Snow	*North Chatham, MA*
A3	Marjorie Haight Lydecker	*Yarmouth Port, MA*
A4	Marjorie J. Farquharson	*Needham, MA*
A5	Marjorie J. Farquharson	*Needham, MA*
B1	Elaine Dwyer	*Centerville, MA*
B5	Sharon Shea	*Plymouth, MA*
C1	Marilyn C. Swenson	*Yarmouth Port, MA*
C5	Lorraine Whitehouse	*Duxbury, MA*
D1	Connie Mooers	*S. Dennis, MA*
D5	Audrey Germer	*Brewster, MA*
E1	Sue Hart	*Norwell, MA*
E2	Sue Hart	*Norwell, MA*
E3	Carrie Thompson	*Wellesley, MA*
E4	Pat Braley	*Acushnet, MA*
E5	Carrie Thompson	*Wellesley, MA*
Center Medallion	Marjorie Haight Lydecker	*Yarmouth Port, MA*
Four Corner Blocks	Marjorie Haight Lydecker	*Yarmouth Port, MA*
Borders	Patricia A. Clayton	*Westborough, MA*
	Dorothy Henion	*Yarmouth Port, MA*
	Marjorie Haight Lydecker	*Yarmouth Port, MA*
	Karen Moraal	*Westborough, MA*
	Marilyn C. Swenson	*Yarmouth Port, MA*
	Audrey Germer	*Brewster, MA*

A2	Terri A. Young	*Monrovia, MD*
	Valeta J. Hensley	*Flemington, MO*
	Suzanne Louth	*Springfield, MO*
A4	Debbie Myler	*Nixa, MO*
A6	Janet Murphy	*Springfield, MO*
B1	Marilynn Bilyeu	*Spokane, MO*
B3	Nancy Hill	*Nixa, MO*
B5	Terri Bozeman-Laird	*Nixa, MO*
B7	Betty K. Bonnot	*Nixa, MO*
Medallion	Suzanne Louth	*Springfield, MO*
	Denise Clausen	*Cloverdale, OR*
C4	Cynthia Catlett	*Springfield, MO*
C6	Jody Martin	*Clever, MO*
D5	Terri A. Young	*Monrovia, MD*
	Valeta J. Hensley	*Flemington, MO*
	Suzanne Louth	*Springfield, MO*
D7	Terri A. Young	*Monrovia, MD*
	Valeta J. Hensley	*Flemington, MO*
	Suzanne Louth	*Springfield, MO*
E4	Missy Hartman	*Ozark, MO*
E6	Valeta J. Hensley	*Flemington, MO*
F1	Harriet Smith	*Springfield, MO*
F3	Joyce Hanson	*Republic, MO*
F5	Katy Conde	*Aurora, MO*
F7	Wanda Davenport	*Springfield, MO*
G2	Terri A. Young	*Monrovia, MD*
	Valeta J. Hensley	*Flemington, MO*
	Suzanne Louth	*Springfield, MO*
G4	Valeta J. Hensley	*Flemington, MO*
G6	D.J. Maas	*Springfield, MO*
X1	Carol Zygadlo	*Ozark, MO*
X2	Carol Zygadlo	*Ozark, MO*
X3	Carol Zygadlo	*Ozark, MO*
X4	Carol Zygadlo	*Ozark, MO*
X5	Maureen L. Ashlock	*Nixa, MO*
X6	Maureen L. Ashlock	*Nixa, MO*
X7	Maureen L. Ashlock	*Nixa, MO*
X8	Maureen L. Ashlock	*Nixa, MO*
X9	Janet Murphy	*Springfield, MO*
X10	Janet Murphy	*Springfield, MO*
X11	Janet Murphy	*Springfield, MO*
X12	Janet Murphy	*Springfield, MO*
X13	Nadine E. Thompson	*Springfield, MO*
X14	Nadine E. Thompson	*Springfield, MO*
X15	Nadine E. Thompson	*Springfield, MO*
X16	Nadine E. Thompson	*Springfield, MO*
Outer Borders	Ruth Rakop	*Newbury, MO*
Corner Compass Blocks	Missy Hartman	*Ozark, MO*

FRIENDSHIP'S OFFERING (QUILT ON page 13)

A1		Deirdre Loughnane	*Calgary, Alberta, Canada*
A3		Sharon H. Aubry	*Calgary, Alberta, Canada*
A5		Joanne Miller	*Calgary, Alberta, Canada*
A7		Mary Lou Zuck	*Cochrane, Alberta, Canada*
A9		Betty Bailey	*Cochrane, Alberta, Canada*
A11		Elizabeth Klingbeil	*Edmonton, Alberta, Canada*
B2		Barbara Gerow Ruault	*Cochrane, Alberta, Canada*
B4		Edith Quinn	*Edmonton, Alberta, Canada*
B6		Dawn Dick	*Stony Plain, Alberta, Canada*
B8		Patti Girling Frostad	*High River, Alberta, Canada*
B10		Nicole Tull	*Edmonton, Alberta, Canada*
C1		Leona Lang	*Williams Lake, British Columbia, Canada*
C3		Laurel Francis-Everett	*Calgary, Alberta, Canada*
C5		Eileen G. Cole	*Cochrane, Alberta, Canada*
C7		Wendy J. Westlake	*Calgary, Alberta, Canada*
C9		Dawn Wakelam Hunt	*Canmore, Alberta, Canada*
C11		Elinor Burwash	*Edmonton, Alberta, Canada*
D2		Dawn Dick	*Stony Plain, Alberta, Canada*
D4		Margaret Geldart	*Victoria, British Columbia, Canada*
D6		Debbie Caseburg Tyson	*Edmonton, Alberta, Canada*
D8		Mary Ann Lohuis	*Calgary, Alberta, Canada*
D10		Evelyn van der Heiden	*Calgary, Alberta, Canada*
E1		Marie E. Collins	*Calgary, Alberta, Canada*
E3		Marcie Lane	*Ajax, Ontario, Canada*
E5		Evelyn van der Heiden	*Calgary, Alberta, Canada*
E7		Sandra Rochon	*Calgary, Alberta, Canada*
E9		Brandis Purcell	*Calgary, Alberta, Canada*
E11		Myrna Shackleton	*Calgary, Alberta, Canada*
F2		Katherine Scott Hudgins Dunigan	*Oakville, Ontario, Canada*
F4		Sandra Smith	*Edmonton, Alberta, Canada*
F6		Terry Aspenlieder	*Calgary, Alberta, Canada*
F8		Zoë Albert	*Chase, British Columbia, Canada*
F10		Joanne Miller	*Calgary, Alberta, Canada*
G1		Leah Gravells	*Edmonton, Alberta, Canada*
G3		Annette E. Johnston	*Red Deer, Alberta, Canada*
G5		Sandra Rochon	*Calgary, Alberta, Canada*
G7		Karen Osatchuk	*Edmonton, Alberta, Canada*
G9		Valerie M. Ursulak	*Nanaimo, British Columbia, Canada*
G11		Zoë Albert	*Chase, British Columbia, Canada*
H2		Elinor Burwash	*Edmonton, Alberta, Canada*
H4		Delores Hill	*Stettler, Alberta, Canada*
H6		Marlene A. Knight	*Edmonton, Alberta, Canada*
H8		Valerie M. Ursulak	*Nanaimo, British Columbia, Canada*
H10		Mary Lou Zuck	*Cochrane, Alberta, Canada*
I1		Lorraine Jacobsen	*Nanoose Bay, British Columbia, Canada*
I3		Bernice Aebly	*Edmonton, Alberta, Canada*
I5		Mary Ann Lohuis	*Calgary, Alberta, Canada*
I7		Sharon E. Green	*Vancouver, British Columbia, Canada*
I9		Andrea Hawkes	*Calgary, Alberta, Canada*
I11		Monica Bishop	*Three Hills, Alberta, Canada*
Border		Leslie J. Barnes	*Calgary, Alberta, Canada*
		Andrea Hawkes	*Calgary, Alberta, Canada*

VERDANT HEARTS (QUILT ON page 15)

A1	B1	C1	D1
A2			D2
A3	Medallion		D3
A4	B4	C4	D4

A1		Susan Kurth	*Oklahoma City, OK*
A2		Marjorie J. Farquharson	*Needham, MA*
A3		Katherine Scott Hudgins Dunigan	*Oakville, Ontario, Canada*
A4		Barbara Phillips-Barrett	*Yountville, CA*
Medallion		Bette F. Augustine	*Hemet, CA*
		Angela Cotter	*Dublin, Ireland*
B1		Lynda Feldman Weingart	*Largo, FL*
B4		Suzanne Louth	*Springfield, MO*
C1		Elinor Burwash	*Edmonton, Alberta, Canada*
C4		Melissa Mattz	*Riverside, CA*
D1		Sue Hart	*Norwell, MA*
D2		Sandra Rochon	*Calgary, Alberta, Canada*
D3		Sheila Patterson Bayley	*Fair Oaks, CA*
D4		Marla Duenwald Landt	*Anchorage, AK*

Courses: Teaching Baltimore Appliqué

Since *Baltimore Beauties and Beyond, Volume One* (C&T Publishing, 1989), Elly has encouraged teaching. Her warm invitation—to laymen and professionals—continues here. Anyone can learn Baltimore appliqué from *Elly Sienkiewicz's Beloved Baltimore Album Quilts* on her own or with a stitching group. Anyone can teach others from it. Your lesson sequence can take its cue from the pattern sequence. In *Elly Sienkiewicz's Beloved Baltimore Album Quilts* the patterns ascend in order from simpler starts to fancy finishes. If you are a beginner at appliqué, you'll be starting just where Elly herself started—on a one-layered appliqué where you cut (only a couple of inches at a time) and sew. Cutaway is simple, yet almost magically effective: Just three pins stabilize the briefly cut area. You appliqué there, then repeat the gentle ritual around the block. Elly designed Pattern 1 for a challenging assignment: to teach all levels in a multilanguage class in Odense, Denmark, without a translator. It worked! Her joy today thrives on the same goal: teaching readers, beginners to advanced, to find their own joy in appliqué. Each of you is a teacher—teaching yourself, some teaching others. This section is for each of you.

Start with Pattern 1

Pattern 1 (Roses for Hans Christian Andersen, page 86) has sixteen look-alike leaves! Repetition is practice. Practice, as we all know, makes perfect! In Cutaway Appliqué (page 32) you pin the block sparingly, then cut a bit, sew a bit. So controlled, so peaceful, you repeat leaf points, curves, and inside corners; gaining confidence, improving your skills, slipping into that secret stitching garden all your own. This gentle repetition of the essentials of appliqué (points, curves, corners) leads you to an heirloom block. It leads from one-layer appliqué to multi-layer, even dimensional, appliqué—all in one pattern. The path is clear; its result is a stunner! Download your free Lesson Plan for this Pattern 1 on www.ctpub.com. Use it for teaching yourself and others in your home, quilt shop, or guild. *Hint:* As you choose a second block to follow Pattern 1, read the notes for each pattern. These notes map pertinent techniques and cite their pages.

Appliqué is like any other skill. Like driving a car, appliqué improves with practice. Starting on a simpler block not only buoys one's confidence but also improves the final quilt. As you stroll through the Gallery (pages 12–22), observe how a simpler block next to a more complex one rests your eye. One shows the other to her best. You'll soon find which technique sets you free—for far from insisting on one *right* way to appliqué, Elly's motto is "Your way is the best way."

Six-Session Beginner-Intermediate Class (Not for Teachers Only)

Fact: Nine blocks makes a near-perfect small quilt (having a natural center block).

Fact: Six 6-hour sessions (or twelve sessions, when split into two 3-hour sessions a month) is near perfect for class commitment in time and cost. With six blocks (or seven if you offer C&T's free download as a prerequisite class) done or well-begun, participants will be ready for a break and then they can finish on their own or take *Elly Sienkiewicz's Beloved Baltimore Album Quilts* Part Two class.

Baltimore Class, Part I: Burst into Baltimore's Beauty! A Beginning Baltimore Class for All

Level: Beginner to Advanced

First Session—Pattern 1: Roses for Hans Christian Andersen

Teach getting started and pattern transfer, tack stitch, Cutaway Appliqué, points, curves, corners, Separate Unit Appliqué with Freezer Paper Inside, Dimensional Appliqué (folded rosebuds), thread, and ink embellishment.

Second Session—Pattern 8: Lyre Wreath in Bloom

Follow the same points, curves, and inside corners learned in the First Session, but the scale is smaller. Both the flower and the optional bird invite a lesson in miniaturization—doing everything the same, but *very carefully* to clarify points, curves, and inside corners. Eye-catching embellishment is a fine finish!

Third Session—Pattern 6: Squirrel's Berry Breakfast

To Cutaway Appliqué (even finer, now!) are added Perfect Circles and a Separate Unit Appliqué squirrel to be done by Freezer Paper Inside with Gluestick; others may prefer to use needleturn to stitch the circles.

Fourth Session—Pattern 19: Spinning Ruched Roses

A minimally marked background, Superfine Stems, tiny leaves by needleturn, or simply fused and edged with blanket stitch. Basic shell ruching for the roses. Ruching is the dimensional glory of Baltimore's Albums!

Fifth Session—Pattern 24: Scalloped Epergne of Fruit

This pattern teaches Separate Unit Appliqué and pattern placement by minimal marking. It asks the use of window templates for evocative print use, or art material appliqué with Liquitex paint products or Sakura's Specialist Oil Pastels (see Sources, page 126).

Sixth Session—Pattern 13: Basket of Flowers

This pattern mixes Cutaway with Separate Unit Appliqué, tying your class start and finish together. "Your way is the best way" reminds us that the buds can be folded, the flowers ruched, the basket woven. With such a grand class finale, why not have the class organize into a friendship stitching group, then back to you for a top-finished graduation party, potluck, … class-organized?

Baltimore Class, Part II:
Turning Baltimore Blocks into a Top!

Show how to lay out a quilt set using 1″ miniatures (from the Patterns section) of the blocks already made. Make a photocopy sheet for each person giving four copies of your block selections for the remaining two to three squares.

■ Explain how an *odd number* of blocks thrives with a center medallion, a nine-block quilt or any other uneven number of blocks has a natural center—one that needs to be chosen carefully. Have students lay out their six (seven if you offer the beginner C&T free download class in addition to the six sessions) blocks and explain their options. Perhaps offer a lesson on any block blown up to be a four-block size for a center medallion, or use the clipper ship pattern.

■ Encourage students to inscribe their quilts or to inscribe a label recording the quilt's provenance to stitch onto the back.

■ For quilting, suggest the option of local machine quilters. Or suggest a hand-quilting class offered by your local shop, one class of which may go into marking, basting, and binding.

■ For ease, use the free class download format for each session's materials and preclass preparations format (www.ctpub.com).

■ Need a quick class model? Cite the lessons pattern page. Use the quilt on page 12 for color models.

■ Need a quilt model to inspire? Paste up, then photocopy for each student a nine-block quilt mock-up out of nine of the 1″ miniatures on each pattern page. Include the six class session blocks. The Family History Block (taught on Elly's beginning Baltimore DVD, *Elly Sienkiewicz Teaches Beginning Baltimore Appliqué*) makes an excellent center and can be learned on one's own with the DVD. It also teaches inscribing, portraiture, and how to make the Dogtooth Border. Include the Star Ruched Rose from Elly's DVD in your mock-up. Putting an asymmetrical block such as this in your quilt's set is like putting a squeeze of lemon juice in your tea! Choose an eighth and ninth block. With sashings, corner blocks, and a Dogtooth Border, you've provided a roadmap to the class.

The Baltimore revival continues, at this book's writing, already three decades long. It continues because we are pulled to beauty. Some of us learn beautifully by ourselves. Others thrive with a good teacher and a supportive class. All over the industrialized world, groups who may have met in guild or in class become, like the Good Ladies of Baltimore, the center of Baltimore Friendship circles that lead to all things good and beautiful.

Thank you for taking this book along on your happy learning journey!

ART MATERIALS FOR APPLIQUÉ

Liquitex Acrylic Paint and Ink
Ask at your local quilt shop or order from C&T Publishing.
800-284-1114
www.ctpub.com

Sakura Specialist Oil Pastels
Dick Blick Art Supplies
800-828-4548
www.dickblick.com

ELLY'S FABRIC AND SUPPLIES FOR APPLIQUÉ
An exquisite new collection of Elly Sienkiewicz Beloved Beauties® fabric is available from P&B Textiles—see the line at www.pbtex.com, for wholesale orders call 800-TLC-BEAR.

Mare's Bears Quilt Shop
302-644-0556; email: maresbears@ce.net
www.maresbearsquiltshop.com

Suzy's Quilts
972-272-8180; email: suzysquilts@aol.com
www.suzysquilts.com

WWW.APPLIQUEWITHELLY.COM
For books (prepublished or self-published, in-print and out-of-print), DVDs, Hanah silk ribbon for stems and baskets, and more. Watch the sales-only website for new debuts.
www.AppliqueWithElly.com

PATTERNS
The Crumpled Wild Rose Spray center medallion or wallhanging, as seen on DVD *Elly Sienkiewicz Teaches Advanced Baltimore Appliqué,* is available from Marjorie Nelson, P.O. Box 6, Frankfurt, MI 49653. email: manj1928@earthlink.net

SHADED WIRED RIBBON

The Find
Sells Offray brand American shaded wired ribbon 1½″; good ribbon but less malleable than the more expensive French shaded wired ribbon. The Find also links to 29 other stores selling wired ribbon.
www.thefind.com/crafts/info-ombre-wired-ribbon

Vintage Vogue
Enticing online store run by nationally known ribbonart designer, Janet Stauffacher; 116 colors in French wire-edge ribbons at an excellent price.
951-279-9115
www.vintagevogue.com

Quilter's Fancy
Small collection of French shaded wired ribbon excellent price.
866-953-0722 toll free
www.quiltersfancy.com

TEACHING INQUIRIES AND WHERE TO FIND ELLY
Elly's once-a-month land and cruisings teaching schedule is posted on www.ellysienkiewicz.com. When contacting her through the website, please enter as the email subject:

"SCHEDULE? Inquiry for Elly. Please just fwd."

Once in a while windows open in a year that appears full. For a quick greeting, watch for her at coffee shops and bookstores in the Washington, D.C., area and at her favorite writer's restaurant, Azafran Café in Lewes, DE.

THE ELLY SIENKIEWICZ APPLIQUÉ ACADEMY
Elly's Annual Appliqué Retreat, ten excellent teachers, one-, two-, and three-day classes. Held every year (mid-February) in temperate Williamsburg, VA, in a beautiful residential hotel, opposite the College of William and Mary. Three-hour lunches allow you to explore Williamsburg's shops, restaurants, and her Abby Aldrich Rockefeller Museum, which owns several real Baltimore Album Quilts. Daily catered social events are more fun than a barrel of monkeys, and never have you seen such Appliqué Show and Tells. Registration opens late July each year. It's never too late to apply, the class you want may still be open.
www.EllySienkiewicz.com

KAREN KAY BUCKLEY'S PERFECT CIRCLES
Sixty assorted-size heat-resistant circles, perfect for Grilled Grapes or use with the Steadfast Gatherer (page 67).
www.karenkaybuckley.com

ULTRASUEDE
The darling of appliquérs. Washable polyurethane synthetic suede— needs no seam allowance added, excellent for fine details such as calyxes, floral centers, eyes, and architectural details.

Fields Fabrics (large selection, retail, reasonable)
www.fieldsfabrics.com > Search "Ultrasuede"
or
www.AppliqueWithElly.com

YLI THREAD SETS FOR APPLIQUÉ AND ORNAMENT
- YLI 100-weight silk, ideal for matching appliqués

- Elly Sienkiewicz Silk 100 Baltimore Album sets in convenient tubes: The Appliqué Travel Set (ES1) and the Classic Appliqué Collection (ES2)

- New! Autumn 2010:

Elly's Embellishments Plain: 5 variegated colors in 30-weight silk embroidery twist.

Elly's Embellishments Fancy: 5 variegated colors in 30-weight silk embroidery twist, plus 2 spools of metallics.

Ornamentation will characterize revivalist Baltimores in the second decade of the twenty-first century!

Ask for YLI thread at your local quilt shop.

Before becoming so deeply involved with group-made Albums, Elly's individual work had been hung at shows across the country and locally at museums and galleries in and around the nation's capital. Inspiring as both a teacher and speaker, she has lectured for the Smithsonian Institution, across the country, and on five continents. Her work is widely published in quilt magazines in the United States, Europe, and Japan; and in *The Magazine Antiques, Folk Art Magazine, Victoria, Country Living,* and *Threads.* Her latest signature fabric lines are showcased on www.pbtex.com. Teaching is

Elly's joy: You'll find her classes filled with tips, techniques, and flower-filled fun!

Elly lives with her husband of 41 years in Washington, D.C. At this writing, her three children live in Afghanistan, New Hampshire, and Vermont. They have blessed their parents with two beloved daughters-in-law and seven grandchildren. Pictured here, waiting for the Mare's Bears quilt shop to open (for borders and backing), are Elly and several avid stitchers among her seven grandchildren.

Also by Elly Sienkiewicz

Appliqué 12 Borders and Medallions
Appliqué 12 Easy Ways
Appliqué Paper Greetings
Baltimore Album Legacy
Baltimore Album Quilts
Baltimore Album Revival
Baltimore Beauties and Beyond, Vol. I
Baltimore Beauties and Beyond, Vol. II

Design a Baltimore Album Quilt
Dimensional Appliqué
Fancy Appliqué
Papercuts and Plenty
The Best of Baltimore Beauties
Romancing Ribbons into Flowers
Spoken Without a Word
Applikationen Ganz Einfach

Great Titles *from* C&T PUBLISHING

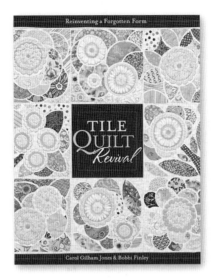

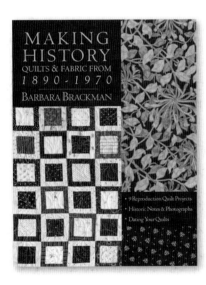

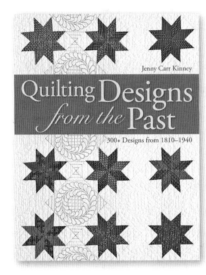

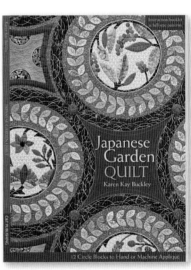

Available at your local retailer or **www.ctpub.com** *or* **800-284-1114**

For a list of other fine books from C&T Publishing, ask for a free catalog:

C&T PUBLISHING, INC.

P.O. Box 1456
Lafayette, CA 94549
800-284-1114

Email: ctinfo@ctpub.com
Website: www.ctpub.com

C&T Publishing's professional photography services are now available to the public. Visit us at www.ctmediaservices.com.

Tips and Techniques can be found at www.ctpub.com > Consumer Resources > Quiltmaking Basics: Tips & Techniques for Quiltmaking & More

For quilting supplies:

COTTON PATCH

1025 Brown Ave.
Lafayette, CA 94549
Store: 925-284-1177
Mail order: 925-283-7883

Email: CottonPa@aol.com
Website: www.quiltusa.com

Note: Fabrics used in the quilts shown may not be currently available, as fabric manufacturers keep most fabrics in print for only a short time.